Psalm 23

McDougal & Associates
Servants of Christ and Stewards of the
Mysteries of God

Psalm 23

A Bird's-Eye View of the Growth of a Christian from This Most Beloved Psalm

BY

PASTOR EMMANUEL UMOSEN

Psalm 23

Cover Design by Robert Charway of Tona Image Studios, Ghana

Published by:

McDougal & Associates
www.thepublishedword.com

McDougal & Associates is dedicated to spreading the Gospel
of the Lord Jesus Christ to as many people as possible
in the shortest time possible.

ISBN 978-1-950398-81-2

Printed in the U.S., the U.K. and Australia
For Worldwide Distribution

DEDICATION

A special dedication to these important people in my life, whose relationship has inspired me to study and write this book. It has been a journey of many years, but through their impartation, encouragement, and unflinching support, the work is finally complete:

The Holy Spirit: who has been my Guide, Wisdom, and Revelation throughout the entire project. I am indeed nothing without Him. With Him, I am everything God created me to be.

The late **Mrs. Angelica Umosen** (AKA: Eka Mama): She was the woman (my grandmother) who showed me the truest, undiluted, sincere, and unconditional love any human can ever give to another. You became both the mother and the father I knew during my formative years. Your instructions still ring loud in my ears, your gentle but firm approach to matters in life still guides my relationships, and your memory remains fresh in my heart.

Minister (Mrs.) Johanna E. Umosen: I call you the wife of my youth. You have been my greatest encourager and a strong support system throughout my adult years. Many times I decided to give up, even on this project, but your wise words, gentle instructions, careful correction, unflinching support, and undying love have kept me going and also brought this project to a successful completion.

My four children (**Emmanuel [Ese], Favor [Ekemini], Joshua [Ubong], and Divine [Emediong]**: Just as mentioned in the first sentence of this book's introduction, your actions during the early part of your lives inspired the writing of this book. It was your use of the words *my* and *mine* that opened my spiritual eyes to the reality of the opening sentence of Psalm 23 – *"The Lord is MY shepherd."* I can honestly say that this project was birthed by your actions around me during your toddler years. You are my heroes for impacting me in such a profound manner that has led to the writing of this book.

SPECIAL THANKS

Special thanks to the following men and women of God for their inspiration, encouragement, design and editing input and prayers:

Apostle Desmond Thomas
The Word International Church
United Kingdom

Pastor Josh Satterfield
Senior Pastor
First at Firewheel (Assemblies of God Church)
Garland, Texas, USA

Pastor Ayodele Adejumobi
Pastor in Charge of Province
The Redeemed Christian Church of God
North America Region 7, Province 2
Edmonton, Alberta, Canada

Pastor Mike Wiggle
Christ Embassy
Houston, Texas, USA

Pastor Magdalene Esi
Senior Pastor
Restoration Ministries of Dallas
Dallas, Texas, USA

Pastor Esosa Ighodaro
Winners Chapel Kansas City
Missouri, USA

Brother Godpower Samuel Beeyah
Dallas, Texas, USA

CONTENTS

FOREWORD BY PASTOR JOSH SATTERFIELD

God expects His children to grow, just like we expect ours to. In this book, Pastor Emmanuel Umosen uses Psalm 23 to beautifully illustrate the stages of development (growth) in a Christian life. This book will help you understand WHO you are and WHOSE you are.

Pastor Umosen has brought out many things that made me stop and think and several that had me shouting, "AMEN!" in my office. I recommend this book to anyone who is looking to be challenged in their walk with Christ.

Pastor Josh Satterfield
Senior Pastor
First at Firewheel (Assemblies of God Church)
Texas, USA

FOREWORD BY PASTOR AYODELE ADEJUMOBI

This is a good book that anyone hungry for growth in their walk with God must read. The author, through the analogy of the Shepherd and His sheep, takes the reader through a step-by-step growth chart in their Christian journey.

This book is also a must for everyone to read in this age in which the world is riddled with identity crises, in which values and gender have become fluid. The book teaches us about our true identity in Christ and how to stand and exercise our authority as believers in the midst of the challenges and vicissitudes of life.

Pastor Ayodele Adejumobi
Pastor in Charge of Province
The Redeemed Christian Church of God
North America Region 7, Province 2
Edmonton, Alberta, Canada

PREFACE BY APOSTLE DESMOND THOMAS

This is one of the finest expositions of the 23rd Psalm you will ever find written. It covers every facet of the Christian life. Pastor Emmanuel Umosen has carefully searched it all out from this beautiful Psalm and exposed it to us in its simplest form. I would recommend the reading of this book more than just to opening your Bible to the 23rd Psalm and putting it under your pillow (which many Christians would like to do). You would profit by reading this book, so read it!

This book exposes the myths and heresies about Christian living now taught by many from their pulpits. It is important that our belief system is right. If we believe right, our practice will be right. This book teaches what is right. In this book, you will come to know the Shepherd more intimately by His attributes and the way He relates to His sheep

(Christians). This book will help you to know the provisions the Shepherd has made for His sheep and how He protects His sheep from all the attacks against them. Pastor Emmanuel teaches us how to respond to the Shepherd's love and provision He has made available to us, which is necessary for our survival in the midst of the troubles all around us.

From this book you will be able to understand the stages of spiritual growth of the Christian. God expects the Christian to grow. He also allows things to happen to us and around us to enable and enhance the growth we need for Christian maturity. Our spiritual growth, Pastor Emmanuel points out, cannot only be fathomed in terms of our walk with God, but also in terms of our growth in ministry. Psalm 23 is key to helping us grow in both dimensions.

This is a balanced book. It will help every genuine Christian who seeks to walk with God in a more perfect way. Full of spiritual wisdom, it is a guide for every babe in Christ who wants to grow into maturity. It will prepare you for what lies ahead in your Christian journey and leave no room for surprises for you in your walk with God.

I encourage every Christian leader to read this book with an open heart, and I assure you that you will be blessed by it. I also encourage every leader to recommend this book for all those who have come to faith in Jesus in their various church groups or Bible study groups. I encourage that it be used to teach Christian growth in every Sunday school. This book has its role to play in the spiritual growth and development of every Christian. Thank you for reading.

Apostle Desmond Thomas
The Word International Church
United Kingdom

AND SAMUEL
GREW, AND THE
LORD WAS WITH
HIM, AND DID
LET NONE OF HIS
WORDS FALL TO THE
GROUND.
— 1 SAMUEL 3:19

INTRODUCTION

The LORD is my shepherd.   Psalm 23:1

My fifteen-year-old son, Ese, when he was just three taught me a lot about the words *my* and *mine*. He would say those words with so much sense of ownership and possession, no matter what the object was, that you began to wonder if you (not he) had really considered the true meaning these words connote.

When Ese said, *"Mine,"* you saw the true sense of the word come to light in his countenance, and he left you with no confusion about whether he meant it or not. In the words of the psalmist, *"The LORD is MY shepherd,"* I have come to realize that although the Lord is the Creator of the entire universe and all there is in it, and as such is saddled with the heavy responsibility of caring for it, when it comes to me, He relates with me as though I am the only thing He created.

The famous country singer, Johnny Cash, wrote "I talk to Jesus every day ... no secretary ever tells me that He's been called away." How could the One who has responsibilities over eight billion people always be available for me 24/7? How could the One saddled with the responsibility of hearing the prayers of over eight billion people be always there for me in my prayer times, no matter how long I choose to pray? How could the Provider of the whole world always be present with me anytime I am in need? Obviously, He must be mine and mine alone first, before that of others, and the same goes for you who are reading this book.

My prayer is that at the end of your reading, you'll realize that there are no problems, issues, obstacles, situations, adversaries, or enemies that are so close to you that the Lord is not closer. May you realize that the Lord, although He is the God of Abraham, Isaac, and Jacob, is your God at the same time, and when He is acting as your Shepherd, there are no ninety-nine others. It's just you and He alone. He will never care for others, listen to the prayers of others, or watch over others at your expense. He is personally there for you anytime, every time, all the time.

Through the Bible, great men have discovered the Lord in diverse ways:

And Moses said unto God, Behold, when I come unto the children of Israel, and shall say unto them, The God of your fathers hath sent me unto you; and they shall say to me, WHAT IS HIS NAME? What shall I say unto them? And God said unto Moses, I AM THAT I AM: and He said, Thus shalt thou say unto the children of Israel, I AM hath sent me unto you.
Exodus 3:13-14
(Emphasis Mine)

And God spake unto Moses, and said unto him, I am the LORD: and I appeared unto Abraham, unto Isaac, and unto Jacob, by the name of God Almighty, but by my name JEHOVAH was I not known to them.   Exodus 6:2-3

God has revealed Himself in diverse ways to diverse people in the Bible. To some, He's been their Ebenezer, to some He's been a Shield and Buckler, to some He's been a Hiding Place, to some a Fountain, an Advocate, the Door, the Way, the Truth, the Light, the Healer, a Defense, the Provider and so on.

In Psalm 23, David, who knew what it took to care for sheep, discovered God as *"MY SHEPHERD,"* knowing full well the benefits one has in being in the Lord. The word *shepherd* refers to a person whose job is to take care of sheep. It means "to tend a flock." Abel is shown as the first shepherd in the Bible:

And Abel was a keeper of sheep.
Genesis 4:2

Rulers were called shepherds:

That saith of Cyrus, He is my shepherd.
Isaiah 44:28

Ministers were called shepherds:

Feed the flock of God which is among you.
1 Peter 5:2

The Lord is called the Chief Shepherd:

And when the chief Shepherd shall appear, ye shall receive a crown of glory that fadeth not away.
1 Peter 5:4

When I call the Lord my Shepherd, it implies that I am a sheep, and so are you, if you have Him as your Shepherd. Sometimes situations arise that seem to throw us into unbelief and a place of just saying the words of Psalm 23 without any real meaning in our hearts. These are the wiles of the devil which work in us to negate all that God is to us.

Sometimes we wonder: "Why did those nasty, bad things happen to Sister A or Brother B or even the pastor of our church? Where was God when those things happened? If He was really there, then perhaps He must not have been acting in the capacity of the Shepherd. If He was, then He must be a very uncaring shepherd." These are important questions, and this book will provide some answers that will help you discover the fullness of the benefits of making the Lord your Shepherd.

At a certain point, years ago, seeing some of the everyday problems and difficulties that some sheep were going through in life raised some of these questions in my own heart. This eventually led me to a desire to write this book, and I pray it will be an answer to someone's questions, a direction to someone's journey, and a way out of someone's confusion.

The truth in the Word of God is that the problem is not with the Shepherd. The Lord is our Shepherd, and I've discovered that He is *"THE GOOD SHEPHERD"*:

Verily, verily, I say unto you, He that entereth not by the door into the sheepfold, but climbeth up some other way, the same is a thief and a robber. But he that entereth in by the door is the shepherd of the sheep. To him the porter openeth; and the sheep hear his voice: and he calleth his own sheep by name, and leadeth them out. And when he putteth forth his own sheep, he goeth before them, and the sheep follow him: for they know his voice. And a stranger will they not follow, but will flee from him: for they know not the voice of strangers. This parable spake Jesus unto them: but they understood not what things they were which he spake unto them.

*Then said Jesus unto them again, verily, verily, I say unto you, I am the door of the sheep. All that ever came before me are thieves and robbers: but the sheep did not hear them. **I am the door: by me if any man enter in, he shall be saved, and shall go in and out, and find pasture.** The thief cometh not, but*

*to steal, and to kill, and to destroy: I am
come that they might have life, and that
they might have it more abundantly.*
*I am the good shepherd: the good shepherd
giveth his life for the sheep.* But he that is an
hireling, and not the shepherd, whose own the
sheep are not, seeth the wolf coming, and lea-
veth the sheep, and fleeth: and the wolf catcheth
them, and scattereth the sheep. The hireling,
fleeth, because he is an hireling, and careth not
for the sheep. **I am the good shepherd**, and
know my sheep, and am known of mine. As the
Father knoweth me, even so know I the Father:
and I lay down my life for the sheep.
And other sheep I have, which are not of this
fold: them also I must bring, and they shall
hear my voice; and there shall be one fold, and
one shepherd. Therefore doth my Father love
me, because I lay down my life, that I might
take it again. No man taketh it from me, but
I lay it down of myself. I have power to lay it
down, and I have power to take it again. This
commandment have I received of my Father.

John 10:1-18 (Emphasis Mine)

As the Good Shepherd, our Lord is
sympathetic:

But when he saw the multitudes, he was moved with compassion on them, because they fainted, and were scattered abroad, as sheep having no shepherd.   Matthew 9:36

As the Good Shepherd, our Lord is gentle and considerate:

He shall feed his flock like a shepherd: he shall gather the lambs with his arm, and carry them in his bosom, and shall gently lead those that are with young.   Isaiah 40:11

As the Good Shepherd, our Lord seeks for the lost:

What man of you, having an hundred sheep, if he lose one of them, doth not leave the ninety and nine in the wilderness, and go after that which is lost, until he find it? And when he hath found it, he layeth it on his shoulders, rejoicing. And when he cometh home, he calleth together his friends and neighbours, saying unto them, Rejoice with me; for I have found my sheep which was lost. I say unto you, that likewise joy shall be in heaven over one sinner that repenteth, more than over

ninety and nine just persons, which need no
repentance. Luke 15:4-7

As the Good Shepherd, our Lord receives
wanderers:

For ye were as sheep going astray; but are now
returned unto the Shepherd and Bishop of your
souls. 1 Peter 2:25

As the Good Shepherd, our Lord protects
and guards:

Now the God of peace, that brought again from
the dead our Lord Jesus, that great shepherd of
the sheep, through the blood of the everlasting
covenant, make you perfect in every good work
to do his will, working in you that which is
wellpleasing in his sight, through Jesus Christ;
to whom be glory for ever and ever. Amen.
Hebrews 13:20-21

As the Good Shepherd, our Lord provides
all our needs:

The LORD is my shepherd; I shall not want.
Psalm 23:1

As the Good Shepherd, our Lord crowns the faithful:

And when the chief Shepherd shall appear, ye shall receive a crown of glory that fadeth not away.   1 Peter 5:4

A sheep, on the other hand, is an animal that always (I mean, always) requires direction. Notice that although people have used phrases such as "like a sheep" in a disapproving way to refer to people who do what others are doing without thinking for themselves, the term *sheep* in the Bible is actually used to distinguish good people from bad people (to sort out or separate the sheep from the goats). Sheep is also used to refer to an honest, humble, meek, and a non-dangerous person. For example, *"a wolf in sheep's clothing"* (Matthew 7:15).

In this present age, when there is so much talk about individual freedom, some, even in the Church, have desired to be free from everything and everybody — including God. Many now justify their riotous living by claiming that this is how they were created (to be free from God) and to indulge in whatever the pleasures of life dictate to them. The

Bible clearly states that God created us for *His* pleasure and not ours:

> *Thou art worthy, O Lord, to receive glory and honor and power: for thou hast created all things* [including me and you], *and for thy pleasure they* [this still includes me and you] *are and were created.*   Revelation 4:11

The Kingdom of God is an autocracy and not a democracy, and God is the King who rules over this Kingdom. God does as He pleases in the armies of Heaven, and on Earth He puts forth His hand, and no man can turn it away:

> *But our God is in the heavens: he hath done whatsoever he hath pleased.*   Psalm 115:3

> *Whatsoever the LORD pleased, that did he in heaven, and in earth, in the seas, and all deep places.*   Psalm 135:6

> *For the LORD of hosts hath purposed, and who shall disannul it? And his hand is stretched out, and who shall turn it back?*
> Isaiah 14:27

And all the inhabitants of the earth are reputed as nothing: and he doeth according to his will in the army of heaven, and among the inhabitants of the earth; and none can stay his hand, or say unto him, What doest thou?

Daniel 4:35

Without God, we can do nothing, and only with Him are all things possible:

I am the vine, ye are the branches: He that abideth in me, and I in him, the same bringeth forth much fruit: FOR WITHOUT ME YE CAN DO NOTHING.   John 15:5
(Emphasis Mine)

But Jesus looked at them and said to them, "With men this is impossible, but with God all things are possible."

Matthew 19:26, NKJV

David, in writing Psalm 23, reminds us that God is all in all, and as the Shepherd, He determines everything that concerns us: where to lie, where to live, what to do, and how to do it. As sheep, we simply FOLLOW, without offering arguments or seeking alternatives.

Psalm 23 reveals that there are levels and dimensions in our walk with God, and the various levels carry unique responsibilities and benefits specific to each level.

Notice that verse 1 of this great Psalm, *"The LORD is my shepherd; I shall not want,"* is carefully omitted from the chapter references of each growth level. This is because the verse stands alone and is not specific to just one of the growth levels; this verse is specific to every level of growth on the chart.

"The LORD is my shepherd; I shall not want" applies to this believer as a newborn babe, but it equally applies to this same believer at the level of taking on Christ's identity. While this believer has grown to the level of operating in the authority of a believer, notice that the Lord remains his Shepherd/Provider. And when this believer grows into locating his place in ministry and even when he enters into God's ultimate manifested presence, the Lord still remains his Shepherd and Provider.

There is absolutely no level on this growth chart that the believer grows out of God's shepherding influence and responsibility. This means you simply never grow out of God's influence and direction.

At any point that the influence and direction of God begins to wane in a believer's life, that believer has simply stopped growing and, instead, has begun to backslide. In the world, the growth and maturity of a child is measured significantly by how much he or she is becoming less dependent on the parent. In the Kingdom economy, the more mature the Christian is, the more dependent on the Lord he becomes.

This book is itself a chronicle by revelation of these levels, and we begin by reading the psalm together, verse by verse from the King James Version of the Bible:

1. *The LORD is my shepherd; I shall not want.*
2. *He maketh me to lie down in green pastures: he leadeth me beside the still waters.*
3. *He restoreth my soul: he leadeth me in the paths of righteousness for his name's sake.*
4. *Yea, though I walk through the valley of the shadow of death, I will fear no evil: for thou art with me; thy rod and thy staff they comfort me.*

5. *Thou preparest a table before me in the presence of mine enemies: thou anointest my head with oil; my cup runneth over.*

6. *Surely goodness and mercy shall follow me all the days of my life: and I will dwell in the house of the LORD forever.*

This psalm provides some insight into the various levels of Christian growth and maturity. The man of God (David), in this most popular of psalms, highlights these levels, which today form a means of measurement for every Christian to determine where they are on this growth chart.

To clearly understand the chart, look at the residential mapping of a particular region in a big city, represented by zip codes. The homes and apartments within the various codes are clearly distinguished in terms of the social status of the residents. Some areas have homes for low income, some for middle income, and others for higher income earners.

Most people simply assume that where they live is the most beautiful there is ... until they decide to take a tour of the entire region. Then the reality hits them, that no matter how high class their current residence is, there is always a zone higher than theirs, with better amenities and infrastructures. Such is the Christian journey.

Understandably, most Christians believe that where they are on this journey is the best and greatest there is, but a careful look into this psalm proves that notion wrong. It is also worth noting that just as people can move or relocate back and forth within certain zones due to economic situations, Christians also move back and forth on this growth chart due to certain spiritual reasons. The direction of their journey can be upward or downward.

Permanent residency in one specific zone is not guaranteed and might also not be a very good idea. No matter how affluent that zone is, there is always a better place to live than your current residence. The Christian journey is ongoing, and the need for growth is constant, for as long as we live on this side of eternity. **THE MOMENT A CHRISTIAN STOPS GROWING, HE STARTS DECAYING!**

In Psalm 23, the man of God breaks down a typical Christian growth chart into various levels, which form the chapters of this book:

1. Newborn Babe (verse 2)
2. Taking on His Identity (verse 3)
3. Operating in the Authority of a Believer (verse 4)
4. Locating Your Place in Ministry (verse 5)
5. His Ultimate Manifested Presence (verse 6)

PSALM 23

LEVEL 5—HIS ULTIMATE MANIFESTED PRESENCE

— VERSE 6 —
Surely goodness and mercy shall follow me all the days of my life: and I will dwell in the house of the Lord forever.

— VERSE 5 —
Thou preparest a table before me in the presence of mine enemies: thou anointest my head with oil; my cup runneth over.

LEVEL 4—LOCATING YOUR PLACE IN THE MINISTRY

— VERSE 4 —
Yea, though I walk through the valley of the shadow of death, I will fear no evil: for thou art with me; thy rod and thy staff they comfort me.

LEVEL 3—OPERATING IN THE AUTHORITY OF A BELIEVER

— VERSE 3 —
He restoreth my soul: he leadeth me in the paths of righteousness for his name's sake.

LEVEL 2—TAKING ON HIS IDENTITY

— VERSE 2 —
He maketh me to lie down in green pastures: he leadeth me beside the still waters.

LEVEL 1—NEWBORN BABE

Through the beautiful Psalm 23, God invites us all to grow.

Pastor Emmanuel Umosen
Wylie, Texas

CHAPTER ONE

NEWBORN BABE

VERSE 2:

He maketh me to lie down in green pastures: he leadeth me beside the still waters.

PSALM 23

LEVEL 5—HIS ULTIMATE
MANIFESTED PRESENCE

— VERSE 6 —
Surely goodness and mercy shall follow me all the days of my life; and I will dwell in the house of the Lord forever.

LEVEL 4—LOCATING YOUR
PLACE IN THE MINISTRY

— VERSE 5 —
Thou preparest a table before me in the presence of mine enemies: thou anointest my head with oil; my cup runneth over.

— VERSE 4 —
Yea, though I walk through the valley of the shadow of death, I will fear no evil: for thou art with me; thy rod and thy staff they comfort me.

LEVEL 3—OPERATING IN THE AUTHORITY OF A BELIEVER

— VERSE 3 —
He restoreth my soul: he leadeth me in the paths of righteousness for his name's sake.

LEVEL 2—TAKING ON HIS IDENTITY

— VERSE 2 —
He maketh me to lie down in green pastures: he leadeth me beside the still waters.

LEVEL 1—NEWBORN BABE

Lying Down

The scriptures clearly identify a group of Christians at this level of the growth chart. 1 Peter 2:2 (NKJV) states:

As newborn babies, desire the pure milk of the word that you may grow thereby.

Notice in verse 2 of psalm 23 that the Bible talks about Christians who seem to have everything working so easy for them that it appears they don't need to do anything for themselves at all. This scripture describes a level on the growth chart where a Christian appears to have life going so smoothly that they don't even need to sit up to eat. They seem to have some element of complete all-the-time calmness in life without experiencing any of the common struggles or disturbances. Everything seems to be coming to them on a golden platter.

This phrase *"maketh me to lie down,"* with the emphasis on lying down, suggest to some extent an act of not having to do anything in order to get whatever you desire. This Christian is not even required to sit up or stand up in order to eat. He can simply eat lying down. He does not even have to walk or work in order to find food. He simply finds himself lying in a bed made of food.

The scripture further describes the Christian at this level on the growth chart as one who has no idea about something called a storm because his journey is always *"beside the still waters."* This Christian has no idea that in the waters of life there are dangerous wild animals present that can pose a threat of danger to his or her life while on this journey.

Shepherds in the Middle East area are said to either lay themselves across running waters to make those waters still for the sheep to drink or to make stone barricades to cause the water to be still so that the sheep can drink. Often, sheep will not drink water that is moving.

There is so much protection given to a babe in Christ by the Shepherd, just as every mother protects a helpless child. Young believers in Christ many times have no sense of danger or of want. Things seem to come to them very easily in their early walk with Christ.

Overflowing Waters

Such a Christian may have no idea that some waters can overflow a person:

And through the rivers, they shall not OVERFLOW thee. Isaiah 43:2
(Emphasis Mine)

They may have no idea that some rivers can overflow their banks and become destructive:

For Jordan overfloweth all his banks all the time of harvest. Joshua 3:15

This verse is revealing. Some rivers seem to be able to choose when to overflow their banks (the time of harvest) in order to cause the greatest impact on a person's life.

These Christians may not even know that seemingly calm and still waters can produce a tempest:

And when he was entered into a ship, his disciples followed him. And behold, there arose a great tempest in the sea, insomuch that the ship was covered with the waves.
Matthew 8:23-24

At this growth level, a Christian may believe that life can be lived on a bed of roses if one is truly in Christ. They may believe that the presence of God implies the absence of storms and that the presence of storms implies the absence of the presence of God. This could not be further from the truth. Even Jesus experienced storms. THE PRESENCE OF STORMS, THEREFORE, DOES NOT IMPLY THE ABSENCE OF THE PRESENCE OF GOD.

A MISCONCEPTION

Even more important, Christians at this level often believe that the only reason others experience storms is because they have strayed from the path of God. This, too, could not be further from the truth. That same verse 23 of Matthew 8 shows that Jesus' disciples *"FOLLOWED Him"* that day. THE PRESENCE OF STORMS DOES NOT NECESSARILY IMPLY THAT A CHRISTIAN HAS STRAYED FROM FOLLOWING CHRIST.

Sadly, this forms the bulk of the New-Age preaching we hear on TV and in many churches these days. As a result, the church is now raising Christians who believe that the absence of storms is a hallmark of Christianity and that all a person needs to do is get born again, and then they can relax and expect life to be cool and dandy all the time.

These Christians believe that God owes them everything, and they owe Him nothing. They believe that Christianity is all about "call it, claim it, and own it," and if, at any time, life goes differently from this belief, it means (in their minds) that either God is absent or the Christian is not following Jesus.

These Christians believe they are entitled to all that God has and that God is never deserving of anything they have. They believe they can whine and complain their way into God's inheritance at any time, and at such time when they cannot have their way, either God doesn't exist or He doesn't love them.

With this forming the bulk of "Gospel" messages we hear nowadays, it is difficult for young Christian converts to understand that Christianity is a race, a lifestyle, and that there are levels of operations as we progress.

In this 23rd Psalm, the psalmist reveals that this stage of Christianity is merely the first level and that there are other levels that exist on the growth chart of our walk/work with God as Christians. As beautiful as life may be at a certain point, the understanding that life is in levels, and there are better levels than where one is currently operating from, creates in us the desire to grow and move to higher and better levels. As good as it sounds to just live life lying down while everything comes to us on a golden platter, we know that there is only one specific period in a natural growth chart when that is absolutely reasonable, and life lived permanently at this level portrays a sense of laziness and dysfunction.

INFANTHOOD

That period is called the infant or newborn level, and it is the responsibility of everyone around us at that time to provide for, cater to, and supply all our needs without expecting anything from us. But, as we grow, it becomes a matter of concern to our caregivers if we continue life at this level and might warrant multiple trips to the doctor's office. If we continue to operate at this same growth level, this becomes an ever more serious health problem the older we get.

What happens? We start losing the function of certain body parts, and we lose muscle mass. The medical field has a name for this phenomenon. It is called *atrophy*, and it means to either use it or lose it. *Atrophy* can be described as "the wasting away of body tissue or an organ,

41

especially as a result of lack of use or under-use." Suddenly, a once healthy individual has hands and legs but cannot use them properly.

This phenomenon can extend to every area of life and not just the body tissues and organs. The skills of an artist can atrophy from lack of use. The ability to retain and deliver the Word of God can atrophy from lack of use. The will power to resist the devil and live right as a believer can atrophy from lack of use. The indwelling desire to be on fire for the Lord can atrophy from lack of use. And this is true for just about every aspect of life.

There was an amazing young child I was blessed to meet many years ago. He was about five or six at the time and was not an ordinary child at all. It was always a mind-blowing experience to see how he operated in ministry. Multiple evangelistic crusades featured this child as the guest speaker, and on each occasion, there were hundreds of souls that answered the altar call to be saved after his preaching.

After some years, when I got an apartment in a certain part of the city, I was surprised to learn that this young man, now no longer a child, was living nearby. It was a shock to think that a child with such potential had been left to roam the streets of this low-income neighborhood just like any other child. He should have been receiving continuous training in ministry. Instead, he was running around with street boys, doing what street boys did, and talking like street boys talked. In short, he had become a complete opposite of the child I had known some eight years before.

When I and other friends came to realize that this was the same young promising evangelist we had known, we began to talk to him often, especially on biblical matters. It turned out that he had completely lost touch with the Scriptures. This boy, who at the age of five or six, had been a walking encyclopedia of the Word of God, had now become empty, as far as the Scriptures were concerned, and it had happened in a period of eight years.

What had happened? The story goes that the parents of this boy, devout Christians themselves, through his gift and those gospel crusades had become very popular and very rich. Then, over the years, they had made multiple bad investment choices and ended up losing their wealth. Coupled with other adversities they encountered during those years, they had developed a deep apathy to the continued training of this child in the way of the Gospel, and at some point, had made the decision to just let him grow up as an ordinary child in the neighborhood.

As the boy continued to neglect the exercise of his spiritual gifts, spiritual atrophy began to set in. At the age of thirteen or fourteen, the boy, who had been such a vibrant evangelist at five and six, had become just like any other child in the neighborhood, with little or no knowledge of the Word of God.

In the realm of the Spirit, living life long term at the first level of the growth chart produces devastating outcomes for Christian children. The seed of greatness, success, and productivity is planted in every born-again Christian at the time of salvation, but that seed is always in the form of POTENTIAL. Please understand that POTENTIAL doesn't always equal reality, at least not automatically. There is a process that must be followed, and there is a cost that must be paid in order to secure the realization of the POTENTIAL. Otherwise it simply atrophies.

In the case of this boy, who at five years of age had the POTENTIAL of becoming the world's leading evangelist, the absence of growth and his continued staying at the same growth level year in and year out led to a complete loss of his ability to retain and effectively deliver the Word of God.

The Christian at Level 1 growth does not know that there are events called droughts, famines, and storms. All he or she knows and has been taught is that the presence of God means the complete absence of these things. Consequently, a Christian child, when faced with droughts, famines, and storms, becomes confused, and is thrown into a state of despondency. He or she believes, at this point, that there are only two options available: 1). Remain at the same level and complain, or 2). Develop unbelief/doubt and return to the world. This child of God is completely oblivious to the fact that there is a third and better option: 3). Moving to the next level on the Christian growth chart.

It is worth noting here that each level on this chart carries responsibilities for the Christian, even the newborn level. The crying of a baby signals the baby's desire. It could be for food, drink, cuddling or comfort, or simply a diaper change. When the baby cries, he or she is telling the parents about an important desire.

Peter wrote, *"As newborn babes, DESIRE the sincere milk of the word, that ye may grow thereby"* (1 Peter 2:2, Emphasis Mine). Peter was admonishing baby Christians to desire. What does that mean? *The Oxford Dictionary* defines *desire* as "to develop and demonstrate a strong feeling of wanting to have something or wishing for something to happen"; "to strongly wish for or want something."

Desire what? At this stage of life, babies drink a lot of milk to further growth. It is advantageous for the newborn Christian to love his milk. He needs to constantly feed on the Word of God for growth to prepare himself for what lies ahead. It is advantageous for the Christian, in the midst of the joy and peace and all the excitements in the discovering of his newfound faith, to understand that these emotions cannot be depended on. Why? Because feelings are not constant. The Christian must continue to feed on the Word, regardless of feelings.

Our Lord Jesus, in the Parable of the Sower, taught that demons (the fowls of the air) come immediately to steal the Word of God from the believer (see Mark 4:3-4), and with time, affliction and persecution arise for the Word's sake, and because of it, many are offended (see Mark 4:17).

DESIRE

Desire is what produces a drive in your life. Every human should be driven by something, and the strength of your drive is directly proportional to the strength of your desire.

Desires produce outcomes in life.
Desires form goals in life.
Desires push one to action.
Desires position one in life for success or failure.
Desires are the bedrock of achievements.

So, Peter instructed the newborn babe in Christ that if there's anything they are required to do, if there is any responsibility on their part, if there is any part they have to play in this Christian race, notwithstanding the fact that he or she is at Level 1, it is simply to DESIRE. Therefore, Peter instructed:

Wherefore laying aside all malice, and all guile, and hypocrisies, and envies, and all evil speakings, as newborn babes, desire the sincere milk of the word, that ye may grow thereby. 1 Peter 2:1-2

These named actions — *malice, and all guile, and hypocrisies, and envies, and all evil speakings* — belong to the former life of sin, and they lead to a separation from fellowship with God. Peter was saying categorically here that even at this Level 1 life on the growth chart, a Christian should be:

- Free from having intentions or desire to do evil — ill will.
- Free from actions or practices of deceiving others by concealing or misrepresenting the truth.
- Free from practices of claiming to have moral standards or beliefs to which his or her behavior does not conform — pretense.
- Free from feelings of discontentment or resentful longing aroused by other's possessions, successes, qualities, or blessings.
- Free from the actions of making false spoken statements damaging to other's reputation.

In order to live free from these things, Peter admonished, the newborn Christian should "*DESIRE the sincere milk of the word*"

(1 Peter 2:2, Emphasis Mine). The Word that caused us to be born again is the same Word that causes growth. Unfortunately, many Christians choose malnourishment instead.

You don't have to command babies to eat; they know when they're hungry. Christians must be reminded that they are spiritually hungry and must be fed. You won't find infants consuming big meals on Sunday expecting that to last them the whole week. Babies eat regularly, taking in nourishment from day-to-day, and Christians need to do the same.

Some believers are consuming spiritual junk food that cannot nourish and will not produce growth. They need a steady diet and application of God's Word instead of man's opinion. Once we taste for ourselves *"THAT THE LORD IS GOOD"* (1 Peter 2:3, NIV, Emphasis Mine), we'll know that nothing else will ever satisfy.

Living Things Grow

The Scriptures clearly provide the main reason for Christians at this level and all levels of the growth chart to feed regularly on the Word of God: *"THAT YE MAY GROW THEREBY"* (1 Peter 2:2, Emphasis Mine).

Living things grow, and growth is a chief characteristic of life. The quality of life itself is measured by the quality of growth, and a Christian who stops growing is a Christian who starts decaying.

As much as life at this first level on the growth chart appears calm, comfortable, and stress free, Christians should note that this is just Level 1, and that there are higher levels of walking with God which can be even more rewarding, comfortable, and secure. Christians should seek to grow out of this newborn babe level as fast as possible in order to fully experience the riches of the glory of God's inheritance in the saints (see Ephesians 1:18).

Paul wrote to the Galatians:

Now I say, That the heir, as long as he is a child, differeth nothing from a servant, though he be lord of all. Galatians 4:1

Just as we desire growth in other aspects of our lives, Christian growth is not optional. It is a necessity as we journey through life as born-again children of God.

Finally, in order to move to the next level on the Christian growth chart, two things are required of the Christian who is at this Level 1, the Newborn Babe. 1). He needs to reject with disdain or contempt–TO PUT OR LAY ASIDE — such things as *malice, guile, hypocrisies, envies, and all evil speaking* (see 1 Peter 2:1). 2). He needs to develop the feeling of intense longing — DESIRE — for the Word of God (see 1 Peter 2:2).

The psalmist agreed:

As the deer pants for streams of water, so my soul pants for you, my God. My soul thirsts for God, for the living God. When can I go and meet with God?   Psalm 42:1-2

The whole duty of the Christian at the Level 1 growth chart is DESIRE, and your desires will determine your movement on the growth chart — upward, downward, or stagnated. I trust that your growth will be forward and upward in Jesus' mighty name. Amen!

CHAPTER TWO

TAKING ON HIS IDENTITY

VERSE 3:
*He restoreth my soul: he leadeth
me in paths of righteousness for his
name's sake.*

PSALM 23

LEVEL 5—HIS ULTIMATE
MANIFESTED PRESENCE

— VERSE 6 —
Surely goodness and mercy shall follow me
all the days of my life: and I will dwell in the
house of the Lord forever.

— VERSE 5 —
Thou preparest a table before me in the
presence of mine enemies: thou anointest
my head with oil; my cup runneth over.

LEVEL 4—LOCATING YOUR
PLACE IN THE MINISTRY

— VERSE 4 —
Yea, though I walk through the valley of
the shadow of death, I will fear no evil:
for thou art with me; thy rod and thy staff
they comfort me.

LEVEL 3—OPERATING IN THE AUTHORITY OF A BELIEVER

— VERSE 3 —
He restoreth my soul: he leadeth me in the
paths of righteousness for his name's sake.

LEVEL 2—TAKING ON HIS IDENTITY

— VERSE 2 —
He maketh me to lie down in green
pastures: he leadeth me beside the
still waters.

LEVEL 1—NEWBORN BABE

The Salvation of Your Soul

When a person gets saved, it is his spirit-man that has been recreated. It is his constant feeding of the Word that saves his soul, which is comprised of his mind, emotions, and will. He has to develop his mind by renewing it with the Scriptures. He must put on the mind of Christ, and he must control his emotions and will and make them subject to the Word of God.

His soul needs restoration. Therefore, he must receive with meekness the engrafted Word which is able to save his soul (see James 1:21). He now has the responsibility to face the challenges to his Christian life and needs to follow in Christ's image and likeness.

Having a Sense of Responsibility

Psalm 23:3 describes the second level of Christian living on the growth chart, which is reflected in the work of the Lord (our Shepherd) in our lives. Here the sheep begins to feel the sense of responsibility as he follows the Shepherd. He soon realizes that the time of continuous LYING DOWN in green pastures is over, and that the Shepherd has clear expectations of him, vis-à-vis how he lives his life.

The Shepherd, for His part, begins to lead us, as the scripture says, in certain paths of life, implying that the sheep is now aware that there are instructions to follow — the DO's and DON'Ts of Christian living. All too often, the sheep now becomes apprehensive about this new level and begins to develop all sorts of thoughts and ideas:

- Some wonder if the Shepherd is still the same as the One on the Level 1 growth chart.
- Some wonder why the Shepherd would suddenly begin to make demands on them.
- Some even wonder if the Shepherd has the right to make such demands.

At this point, the sheep is faced with three options:

1. Remain in the fold at this same level,
2. Remain in the fold but go back to the first level (living life as a newborn babe), or
3. Drop out of the sheepfold altogether.

This, you see, is what happens to us as we seek better zip codes to live in. Some, upon discovering that the new residential area has greater demands and higher costs, decide to either remain and shoulder the responsibilities, pack up and move back to the cheaper zip code they came from, or just flat out move out of the region or state entirely.

The sheep's challenge, at this level, is further complicated by the actions (or lack thereof) and preaching (or lack thereof) of the men of God over them.

LIVING FOR HIM

When all a young Christian hears about is the "Gospel" of "once saved, always saved," that God doesn't see, let alone care about what you do once you're born again, and that the measure of Christian growth is more in the material than in the spiritual, this Christian suddenly finds himself thrown from a state of heightened excitement, as a result of his new birth, into a state of utter despondency, confusion, and perplexity from the demands of the second growth level of his Christian living.

When this young Christian learns that the time of continuous LYING DOWN in green pastures is over, and it's time to get up and begin to follow some leading, he suddenly discovers that he can no longer follow ALL THE PATHS OF LIFE laid out before him. The Shepherd has chosen a SPECIFIC PATH that he must now follow. *"He leadeth me in the paths of righteousness."*

The young Christian suddenly discovers that he was saved for the Shepherd and not for himself, and that all things were not only created *by* Him, but that they were also created *for* Him as well:

> *For by him were all things created, that are in heaven, and that are in the earth, visible and invisible, whether they be thrones, or dominions, or principalities, or powers: all things were created by him and for him.* Colossians 1:16

The young Christian suddenly learns that the Shepherd already had his path laid out even before he became born again and that the Shepherd will not accept anything less from him, whether the preacher has spelled it out or not. Note this scripture:

> *For we are his workmanship, created in Christ Jesus unto good works, which God has before prepared that we should walk in them.* Ephesians 2:10

Recreated to Do Good Works

Notice that the work here must qualify as GOOD WORK by the Shepherd's own standard and that these works were created (spelled out) even before you were born again, even though the preacher might not have informed you during that evangelistic crusade where you made your decision for Christ during that altar call.

Just as the government administrators in the new, better neighborhood would not change the city or district laws governing that zip code simply because the guy who sold you your new home didn't spell them all out, the Shepherd does not excuse the sheep from following THE PATH OF RIGHTEOUSNESS simply because the preacher did not preach it to you to begin with.

Membership in This Kingdom Family Is by Adoption.

Having predestinated us to adoption as sons by Jesus Christ to himself, according to the good pleasure of his will.   Ephesians 1:5

Let's say that the Jones family goes out and adopts a child and brings that child home. At the first phase, nobody cares about the child's past or potential inherent traits. Everyone simply celebrates the child the way he or she is.

However, after this comes the second phase. Now Mr. and Mrs. Jones begin to instruct and lead the child in the ways of the Jones family. They begin to instill into the child some new specific traits of the Joneses, knowing that this child has taken up the Jones' family name and that going forward, whatever the child does or fails to do will be directly accredited or attributed to the Jones' family name.

One thing most adoptees struggle with is identity. Part of our identity is formed at birth, but the bulk of it is formed during adolescence. It is our identity that enables us to know the things about us that are consistent and unique from others. Many experiences and events help mold how we see ourselves as we grow up and, for adoptees, the process can be somewhat difficult.

An adopted child, to some extent, leaves some part of himself/herself behind, and this includes a different life that the child might have had if he/she had not been adopted. This means that there is an adoptive identity the child must begin to take on after being adopted.

Please understand that identity formation can be a very confusing, frustrating, and
sometimes difficult and painful process for
an adoptee. The adolescent, before his/her
adoption into the new family, already had
many things going on in his/her life, and being suddenly introduced to new parents with
separate rules and probably different cultures
could create many questions without answers,
thus leading to identity confusion. This can af-
fect a child's emotional stability. The child, if
unable to properly form the new identity, can
begin to have a sense of loss, thereby develop-
ing problems in relationships and creating an
overall sense of insecurity. It is important for
the adoptee to be raised in a well nurtured en-
vironment in order to successfully adapt to the
practices, culture, and lifestyle of the adopted
family.

Likewise, the Shepherd, in verse 3 of the
23rd Psalm, begins to lead (nurture, guide, instruct) the sheep in the paths particular only to
the Shepherd — PATHS OF RIGHTEOUSNESS.
He does this, not for the "NAME SAKE" of
the sheep or where he was adopted from, but
"FOR HIS [the Shepherd's] NAME'S SAKE."
He does this so that the sheep can successfully

develop the new adoptive identity, the identity of the Shepherd.

Just as the Joneses have to lead the adopted child in the ways of the Jones family, it is imperative that the Shepherd begins to lead the sheep in the ways of His family (*the paths of righteousness*), hence the phrase "becoming like Jesus."

A young girl was adopted into a Christian family by a lady whose husband had passed away a few years before. Sadly, the lady died while the adopted girl was still very young and had not fully adapted to the Christian culture and practices of the adopted family. The extended family of the adoptive mother decided to take the young girl because their sister (the adopted mom) had passed away. But the extended family, while wanting to keep the girl, demanded that the original adopted family maintain financial responsibility for the girl's upbringing. They were willing to oblige ... until they realized that the adopted girl was beginning to engage in practices and a lifestyle which were totally inimical to the interests and Christian culture and values of the original adopted family.

At this point, the adopted family members demanded that the girl be returned to them so they could effectively nurture her in the family's Christian tradition and culture, while carrying out their financial responsibilities. They became insistent because the girl bore the family name, and they feared that her bad life-style would bring shame to the family name she still represented. Therefore, for the sake of the family name, they had the girl returned to them so she could be led (instructed, guided, taught) in the path of the family's Christian culture and tradition (righteousness).

After being returned to the family, the girl was enrolled in a Christian school, and with close interaction with the rest of the family members, she was completely transformed over the next several years. Thankfully, she is now living a good, happy Christian life, just like the rest of the members of her original adopted family.

Abraham had an adopted son:

And Abram said [to God]: *Behold, to me thou hast given no seed* [biological child]: *and lo, one born* [raised, nurtured, trained, taught] *in my house is mine heir.*   Genesis 15:3

Abraham considered Eliezer as an adopted child and was willing to allow him to inherit his wealth after his death, However, the striking truth in this scripture is not just that of inheritance, but the fact that Abraham considered Eliezer a potential heir just because he (Eliezer) had been born (raised, nurtured, tutored, instructed, guided, trained) in his (Abraham's) house. The important truth here is that an adopted child needs to grow and be raised by the adopted family in order to fully imbibe the culture and tradition of his/her adopted family. He/she needs to be raised by the adopted family in order to successfully take on the new identity, that of the adopted family.

Abraham had many servants, but he was willing to make Eliezer his heir, meaning he now considered Eliezer as an adopted son. His reasoning was that Eliezer was *"ONE BORN IN MY HOUSE."* Abraham believed that Eliezer had taken on the identity of his family since he had been born (raised, taught, nurtured, instructed, and guided) in his house. Eliezer could not have been adopted into Abraham's family if he had been nurtured and tutored somewhere else.

Likewise, it is expected by God that after our adoption into His Kingdom, we be nurtured, tutored, and guided in the House of God. The Christian cannot continue to be nurtured and tutored outside the House of God. He cannot continue to be raised in clubs and gangs and pagan associations while, at the same time, claiming adoption into the Kingdom of God.

It becomes imperative for the born-again Christian (adopted by God) to grow up, be trained and nurtured in the Church, and to have good Christian teachers and instructors who will help him grow spiritually, fully adopting the identity of Christ. It becomes very important for the young Christian to be fully involved in the day-to-day, week-to-week, month-to-month, and year-to-year activities of the new family (the Church). God's Word declares:

Not forsaking the assembling of ourselves together, as the manner of some is; but exhorting one another: and so much the more, as ye see the day approaching.　　Hebrews 10:25

HEIRS OF GOD.

The Scriptures also declare that as children of God we are *"heirs of God, and joint heirs with*

Christ" (Romans 8:17). By adoption through faith in God, we become joint heirs with Jesus. Praise the living God! We become inheritors of the Kingdom prepared for us from the foundation of the world (see Matthew 25:34). Praise the Lord!

This is the heavenly Kingdom (see 2 Timothy 4:18), and this is an inheritance that is incorruptible, undefiled and does not fade away (see 1 Peter 1:4). Praise God!

God's Kingdom is for those who are its heirs, and heirs are those who are chosen by God by adoption through faith in Christ Jesus, those who are rich in faith and love the Lord (see James 2:5).

Christians should understand that although we are not saved by good works, we are indeed saved unto (for) good works:

And the world passeth away, and the lust thereof: but he that doeth the will of God abideth forever.   1 John 2:17

So, get rid of your old self, which made you live as you used to, the old self that was being destroyed by its deceitful desires:

And you must put on the new self, which is created in God's likeness and reveals itself in the true life that is upright and holy.

Ephesians 4:24, GNT

Not everyone that saith unto Me, Lord, Lord, shall enter into the kingdom of heaven; but he that doeth the will of my Father which is in heaven. Many shall say to me in that day, Lord, Lord, have we not prophesied in thy name? and in thy name cast out devils? and in thy name done many wonderful works? And then will I profess unto them, I never knew you: depart from me ye that work iniquity. Matthew 7:21-23

But be ye doers of the word and not hearers only, deceiving your own selves. James 1:22

What doth it profit, my brethren, though a man say he hath faith, and have not works? Can faith save him? If a brother or sister be naked, and destitute of daily food, and one of you say unto them, Depart in peace, be ye warmed and filled; notwithstanding ye give them not those things which are needful to the body; what doth it profit? Even so faith, if it hath not works, is dead, being alone.

Yea a man may say, Thou hast faith, and I have works: shew me thy faith without thy works, and I will shew thee my faith by my works. Thou believeth that there is one God; thou doest well: the devils also believe, and tremble. But wilt thou know, o vain man, that faith without works is dead? Was not Abraham our father justified by works, when he had offered Isaac his son upon the altar? Seest thou how faith wrought with his works, and by works was faith made perfect? And the scripture was fulfilled which saith, Abraham believed God, and it was imputed unto Him for righteousness: and he was called the friend of God. Ye see then how that by works a man is justified, and not by faith only.
Likewise also was not Rahab the harlot justified by works, when she had received the messengers, and had sent them out another way? For as the body without the spirit is dead, so faith without works is dead also.

James 2:14-26

Who is a wise man and endued with knowledge among you? let him shew out of a good conversation his works with meekness of wisdom.

James 3:13

Let us be glad and rejoice, and give honour to him: for the marriage of the Lamb is come and his wife hath made herself ready. And to her was granted that she should be arrayed in fine linen, clean and white: for the linen is the righteousness of saints.   Revelation 19:7-8

In all things shewing thyself a pattern of good works: in doctrine shewing uncorruptness, gravity, sincerity.   Titus 2:7

Who gave himself for us, that he might redeem us from all iniquity, and purify unto himself a peculiar people, zealous of good works.   Titus 2:14

Put them in mind to be subject to principalities and powers, to obey magistrates, to be ready to every good work.   Titus 3:1

This is a faithful saying, and these things I will that thou affirm consistently, that they which have believed in God might be careful to maintain good works. These things are good and profitable unto men.   Titus 3:8

And let our's also learn to maintain good

works for necessary uses, that they be not un-fruitful.   Titus 3:14

In the letters to the churches in Revelation chapters 2 and 3, we read over and over, *"I know your works"* (see Revelation 2:2, 9, 13 and 19, 3:1, 8 and 15). God is interested in us doing the work He has prepared for us, and this is the only thing that produces any weight on His scale.

I saw a sign in a pastor's office some time ago that read: **"God formed man, sin deformed man, and Christ transforms man."** The Bible evolution of man is that man was created (formed) in God's image, in the beginning:

> *So God created man in his own image, in the image of God created he him; male and female created he them.*   Genesis 1:27

Man became deformed by sin:

> *But of the tree of the knowledge of good and evil, thou shalt not eat of it: for in the day that thou eatest thereof thou shalt surely die.*
>   Genesis 2:17

And when the woman saw that the tree was good for food, and that it was pleasant to the eyes, and a tree to be desired to make one wise, she took of the fruit thereof, and did eat, and gave also unto her husband with her; and he did eat. And the eyes of them both were opened, and they knew that they were naked; and they sewed fig leaves together and made themselves aprons.

And they heard the voice of the LORD *God walking in the garden in the cool of the day: and Adam and his wife hid themselves from the presence of the* LORD *God amongst the trees of the garden.* Genesis 3:6-8

Next, man in his sinful nature began to produce offspring, no longer in God's image, but in his (man's) fallen image. Notice the difference between Genesis 5:1 and 5:3:

This is the book of the generations of Adam. In the day that God created man, <u>in the likeness of God made he him</u>. Genesis 5:1
(Emphasis Mine)

And Adam lived an hundred and thirty years, <u>and begat a son in his own likeness, and after</u>

his image; and called his name Seth.
Genesis 5:3
(Emphasis Mine)

Finally, God sent His Son (Jesus Christ) into the world so that man would be transformed back into the image and likeness of God:

Therefore as by the offence of one judgment came upon all men to condemnation; even so by the righteousness of one the free gift came upon all men unto justification of life. For by one man's disobedience many were made sinners, so by the obedience of one shall many be made righteous.   Romans 5:18-19

Nevertheless when it shall turn to the Lord, the veil shall be taken away. Now the Lord is that Spirit: and where the Spirit of the Lord is, there is liberty. But we all, with open face beholding as in a glass the glory of the Lord, are changed into the same image from glory to glory, even as by the Spirit of the Lord.   2 Corinthians 3:16-18

The purpose of God adopting us is for us to have a family, a fold, and the uniqueness of the family system lies in its homogeneity, which is the state of being all of the same kind. God is holy, and they who worship and follow Him must be like Him. Hence He leads us in the paths of righteousness (who He is) *"FOR HIS NAME'S SAKE."*

Because we take on His name after being born again, what we do out there reflects heavily on Him.

CREATED IN RIGHTEOUSNESS AND HOLINESS

But of him are ye in Christ Jesus, who of God is made unto us wisdom, and righteousness, and sanctification, and redemption.
                              1 Corinthians 1:30

In Chapter 1, we talked about the phrase *"I shall not want."* Our Shepherd in our new creation has endowed us with everything we need to live a prosperous Christian life. We shall not want any good thing. Our righteous Shepherd does not require of us what He has not created us to be. That would be an unlawful demand. He created us in wisdom, righteousness, sanctification, and redemption. The Shepherd created us in Himself with the ability for wisdom, righteousness, sanctification, and redemption.

Every true believer in Christ possesses the ability to live in holiness and righteousness, to live a life of redemption from sin and the forces of darkness. No believer should have any quarrel with walking in holiness and righteousness. Why? Because this ability is created in us at our new birth. No believer should make any excuse that the devil made them do something because they are created with the power of redemption from sin, the devil, and the world. So every Christian should first accept their new creation status, that of holiness and righteousness, and then begin to walk in the newness of their life.

Don't try to be holy; you are holy. Don't try to be righteous; you are righteous. Don't try to get redemption from Satan, sin, and the world; you are already delivered from them. What you need to do now is walk in your newness of life:

Therefore we are buried with him by baptism into death: that like as Christ was raised up from the dead by the glory of the Father, even so we also should walk in newness of life.

Romans 6:4

PATHS OF HOLINESS AND RIGHTEOUSNESS

The Bible says that the disciples of Jesus were *"called Christians first in Antioch"* (Acts 11:26). Why? I believe the people of that day took time to watch how the disciples lived their lives, how they related and interacted with each other and the outside world, and over time concluded that these men and women acted just like the Shepherd and were following the same paths (the paths of righteousness) as the Shepherd.

God expects us to become like Christ, and the second level in the growth chart is where the Shepherd begins a specific work in us after the new birth, a work that, if we yield to it, will make us mature to walk like Him. God expects every Christian to walk in holiness and righteousness for the sake of His name:

But as he which hath called you is holy, so be ye holy in all manner of conversations; because it is written, Be ye holy; for I am holy. And if ye call on the Father, who without respect of persons judgeth according to every man's work, pass the time of your sojourning here in fear.
                              1 Peter 1:15-17

The Christian, at this level, in order to grow, must add submission to his desire. The Shepherd alone is the Guide and the desire of the child of God and the constant prayer of the Christian at this level is that God would lead, guide, and also grant the wisdom to submit to His leading:

He that hath clean hands, and a pure heart; who hath not lifted up his soul unto vanity, nor sworn deceitfully. He shall receive the blessing from the LORD, *and righteousness from the God of his salvation.*

Psalm 24:4-5

Teach me, and I will hold my tongue: and cause me to understand wherein I have erred.

Job 6:24

Lead me, O LORD, *in thy righteousness because of mine enemies, make thy way straight before my face.*

Psalm 5:8

Teach me thy way, O LORD, *and lead me in a plain path, because of mine enemies.*

Psalm 27:11

For thou art my rock and my fortress; therefore for thy name's sake lead me, and guide me.
                                    Psalm 31:3

Teach me thy way, O LORD; I will walk in thy truth: unite my heart to fear thy name.
                                    Psalm 86:11

Make me to go in the path of thy command-ments; for therein do I delight. Psalm 119:35

To him the porter openeth; and the sheep hear his voice: and he callest his own sheep by name, and leadeth them out. And when he putteth forth his own sheep, he goeth before them, and the sheep follow him, for they know his voice.
                                    John 10:3-4

The duty of a Christian at this Level 2 on the growth chart is to add submission to his Level 1 duty of desire. Your submission determines your movement on the growth chart — upward, downward, or stagnated. I trust that your spiritual growth, beloved, shall be forward and upward in Jesus' mighty name. Amen!

CHAPTER THREE

OPERATING IN THE AUTHORITY OF A BELIEVER

VERSE 4:

Yea, though I walk through the valley of the shadow of death, I will fear no evil: for thou art with me; thy rod and thy staff they comfort me.

PSALM 23

LEVEL 5—HIS ULTIMATE MANIFESTED PRESENCE

— VERSE 6 —
Surely goodness and mercy shall follow me all the days of my life: and I will dwell in the house of the Lord forever.

— VERSE 5 —
Thou preparest a table before me in the presence of mine enemies: thou anointest my head with oil; my cup runneth over.

LEVEL 4—LOCATING YOUR PLACE IN THE MINISTRY

— VERSE 4 —
Yea, though I walk through the valley of the shadow of death, I will fear no evil: for thou art with me; thy rod and thy staff they comfort me.

LEVEL 3—OPERATING IN THE AUTHORITY OF A BELIEVER

— VERSE 3 —
He restoreth my soul; he leadeth me in the paths of righteousness for his name's sake.

LEVEL 2—TAKING ON HIS IDENTITY

— VERSE 2 —
He maketh me to lie down in green pastures; he leadeth me beside the still waters.

LEVEL 1—NEWBORN BABE

Divine Authority

The third level on the Christian growth chart is marked by a clear understanding and manifestation of divine authority. At this level, the same Christian who would only be led beside waters that are still (no storms) in Level 1, and the same Christian who thought, in Level 2, that all the Shepherd's leading was simply in paths of righteousness, suddenly learns that the Christian race involves valleys of the shadow of death. Now the Christian learns that even the roses in the Level 1 growth chart have thorns. He discovers that the waters produce storms and floods, even tempests and that the green pastures sometimes disappear due to floods or droughts.

The believer also finds that there are giants on the way to hinder and provoke fear. He finds that there is not only morning, but there is also night where and when weeping endures. He finds that the Christian race is one of WAR against enemies bigger than flesh and blood. He finds that there is a sophisticated kingdom that is against his or her survival as a Christian, against his or her survival as a couple, against his or her survival as a career person, against his or her survival as a parent, against his or her survival in terms of health, finances, and general wellbeing.

THE AGE FOR WAR

The Israelites had a set age when a child was considered an adult and ready for war. Ancient Greeks and other ancient tribes would put their young men through tests to train and prepare them for warfare. Why? It was time for that young adult to understand warfare, time for that young adult to understand the disciplines of war, time for that young man to understand the morals, ranks, and authority in the disciplines of that army. It was time for maturity.

There was a common parental practice that was prevalent back in the time when my late father was a young child. The same story was told by my elderly maternal uncle about his growing-up days and it seems to fit the same experience my father had.

The two families were very rich and industrious and had made a name for themselves in the area of commerce. In the case of my late father, his father was a very successful and wealthy businessman, and his mother was a successful farmer. My father was their only child, and as such, was very pampered by his parents, making him look like a typical Level 1 growth Christian in the 23rd Psalm. Both parents were Christians, and they had all the resources they needed to raise and train him, but at some point they realized that their only son was becoming spoiled and not maturing well. He still needed others to do virtually everything for him at an age when he should have been doing them for himself. Every attempt by the parent to correct this behavior and help my father mature more quickly failed. He continued to believe that his parents' love for him was demonstrated strictly in how many luxuries they provided for him in his worry-free life.

At some point, the parents became worried because their only son was not maturing properly and decided to send him to live with a head teacher back in the village, so that he could learn discipline and be prepared for the next phase of his life.

These school head teachers were the greatest disciplinarians of the time, and every child dreaded being raised by them. They were somewhat poor and lacked most basic amenities for an easier lifestyle. For example, they couldn't afford a kerosene cooking stove at the time and had to burn firewood each time they prepared a meal. Just this practice alone was a very tough way to live because someone had to constantly blow air from their mouth into the fire in order to keep it burning, while the meal was being cooked.

The school head teachers at the time also could not afford to have water from a well, so someone, usually their children, had to walk miles to the village stream every day to fetch water for the family. This water had to be carried back home in containers on their head, not in some mobile equipment like a truck or even a wheelbarrow.

My grandparents, at some point, decided that it was in my father's best interest to send him to live with the village head teacher, to deny him most of the luxuries and pampering he was accustomed to at the time, and to allow him to experience some tough situations in life. He needed to change his concept of life and to grow into a mature man, ready to face the challenges of life without giving up on himself because of the storms of life.

The story goes that my grandparents were actually paying the school head teacher some monthly stipend for him to train their son in the ways of life. My father considered this to be very mean, and it was a difficult time for him.

In the case of my uncle, I am told that on one occasion, his parents visited him at the head teacher's house and found him blowing air onto the firewood while a meal was being cooked. My uncle's eyes were all red from the smoke, and to make things worse, the head teacher was just relaxing in his chair, waiting for his meal to be served. At this point, my maternal grandma couldn't help but shed tears, seeing her loving son go through that experience. Still, they continued with the arrangement and did not take him home that day.

My uncle concluded that the parents were very mean to him, to allow him go through those experiences when they had enough resources to provide him comfort and luxury. He concluded that his parents just didn't care at all. My father reacted much the same way, considering his parents to be mean, wicked, absentee parents.

In the end, both my late father and my uncle grew up to become very successful in life, and both came to the same conclusion — that their success in life was a result of the tough, painful, situations they had gone through at the hands of those head teachers. They realized that while they went through those tough times, their parents were never really absent from their lives. They were always there to ensure that they became successful in life, to ensure that they became victorious in life's battles. Their parents had not withheld needed resources from them, but were still spending money and making great sacrifices for them, so they could emerge ready to take on life's situations and circumstances with confidence and calm.

That reminds me of a story I heard some time ago about the formation of an eagle. Every action of the young eagle (they're called eaglets) is overseen by the parents. They supply constant and adequate food, comfort, warmth, safety, etc. as long as the eaglet remains in the nest. At some point, however, the eagle realizes that her baby, if allowed to remain at this Level 1 growth, will never grow up to become a true eagle.

Eagles are fierce birds that thrive where other birds dread to go. These birds are not intimidated by the strength and size of their prey. They are highly tenacious birds with great vitality, and they fly at great heights.

To bring her eaglet to maturity, the eagle begins a training program for her little one. She takes the eaglet from the nest (his comfort zone), carries him up in the air and then releases him there. One wonders what must be going through the mind of that eaglet as he tumbles down through the air, the wind beating on his body, and he looks down to what appears to be an imminent crash to the ground.

At this point, the eaglet must be thinking: "What a wicked bird my once-loving mother has become! What an absentee mom my formerly always-present mom has become! What an uncaring mom my once-super-caring mom has become!" But, just at the point when the eaglet is about to hit the ground or a hard rock, the mom sweeps in, picks him up, and flies right up into the skies with him again.

At this point, the eaglet is thinking: "Mom, why would you make such a mistake with your beautiful and fragile baby? Don't you care that he was about to die?"

At the same time, while the eaglet is having some sense of relief, the mom goes way up in the sky and then suddenly releases the eaglet again. This program continues for days until, at some point, the eaglet's wings become strong enough and agile by reason of the storms and the winds, and he finds that he can fly on his own. Through tough training, he has become a mature eagle, a bird that hunts and yet cannot be hunted, a bird of great power and strength, a bird that has mastered the techniques of stability in the midst of every storm.

In the end, the eaglet that cursed his mom for allowing him to go through such storms, now realizes that the mom allowed it all to prepare him for a great life ahead. She needed him to mature and move on to the next level of life.

There is, therefore, the age for war: *"Yea, though I walk through the valley of the shadow of death, I will fear no evil."* Christians need to understand that there is a thing called spiritual warfare. Christianity is a battle, there are enemies of your faith, and there are valleys and shadows of death to be faced. Christians need to understand that fears will try to overwhelm you, but that God has not given you the spirit of fear but of power and of love and of a sound mind (see 2 Timothy 1:7).

The Christian needs to know Who leads in this warfare, and he needs to trust in His rod and staff for comfort in the midst of the valleys and shadows of death. The Christian must understand that in warfare there will be casualties, both spiritual and physical. And the warfare only gets worse when there is no trust in the Shepherd's rod and staff.

The Christian now discovers what he probably wasn't taught, that this race that began so well at Level 1, with him not having to do much to succeed, requires more than desire and submission. He discovers that although the preacher failed to mention that the journey he was about to begin would lead him to mountains and valleys, days and nights, these things are very real.

He now learns about a man from the land of Uz called Job, a man the Scriptures conclude was *"perfect and upright, and one that feared God, and eschewed evil"* (Job 1:1). This man would come to a place where he had to sigh even in the face of good food placed before him:

For my sighing cometh before I eat, and my roarings are poured out like the waters.

Job 3:24

The Christian now learns that this perfect and upright brother, Job, still came to a point in life that he and his spouse wished each other dead (see Job 2:9), and his close friends mocked and disdained him and each other (see Job 4:1-9).

The Christian soon learns that this perfect and upright brother, Job, who was the greatest of all the men of the East, still came to a moment in the race when he suffered the loss of everything he had worked and labored for. He learns that there is an enemy capable of sowing tares among the wheat (the green pastures) of the believer:

> *But while men slept, his enemy came and sowed tares among the wheat and went his way.*   Matthew 13:25

Now the Christian discovers that there were moments during Jesus' race, when He, Who knew that He and the Father were one, would have to ask the Father *"Why hast thou forsaken me?"* (Matthew 27:46). Why? Because of the intensity of the battle, the pain, the afflictions, and the loneliness of it all. This is where many Christians begin to wonder if God truly exists and why bad things seem to happen to good people.

This feeling is more clearly displayed in the 73rd Psalm, where David concluded in verse

1 that *"God is good"* and yet began to slip into unbelief when he began to wonder and ponder why bad things happen to good people. He philosophized in verse 5 that the good people seemingly are the ones always in trouble and the wicked are not:

> *They* [the wicked] *are not in trouble as other men; neither are they* [the wicked] *plagued like other men.* Psalm 73:5

This third growth level reveals that the Christian race is not a bed of roses, but it also reveals that we can be and are destined to be overcomers in this world. This level reveals that the Christian is:

> *Troubled on every side, yet not distressed; ... perplexed, but not in despair; persecuted, but not forsaken; cast down, but not destroyed.*
> 2 Corinthians 4:8-9

JESUS PROMISED THAT WE ARE OVERCOMERS

> *These things I have spoken unto you, that in me ye might have peace. In the world ye shall*

have tribulation: but be of good cheer; I have overcome the world. John 16:33

A man I know grew up in rejection, abuse, and neglect by his earthly father and step-mom. Nothing he did as a young child was good enough in the eyes of his earthly father. He was constantly beaten and screamed at, was denied adequate attention and supplies of basic needs, even for his schooling. While a child, he was also denied a relationship with his birth mother, simply because the father hated her so much.

This father, when the boy's mother, duly married to him, was pregnant with the boy, had become separated from his wife because of the war that was being waged in that region of the world at the time. The man worked in government, so he needed to stay in the city, but they agreed that the wife should go to the village and live with his mother where it was safer. He would join her there later.

In time, the wife gave birth to her son. Unfortunately, because they were separated for some time, the husband took up with another woman, and when he finally arrived, he had the other woman with him and insisted that he was taking a second wife.

Not surprisingly, tension arose between the two women, and at some point, the mother made the decision to quit the marriage, refusing to be involved in polygamy. It was at this point that her husband developed his hatred toward her.

It appears that the hatred for the woman was transferred to her child. The stepmother would not accept the child as a lawful member of the family and saw him as a threat to her inheritance because she was not able to bear a child of her own for her husband. She, therefore, ensured throughout the years of the child growing up, that the father hated and maltreated him, to the point that it became unbearable for the child to remain in the home. He had to move out and fend for himself at an early age.

This young man got saved and committed his life to God. He fought to keep a level head while struggling through life, and with the help of an uncle, was able to go to college, graduate, and became successful.

The man was later able to restore his relationship with his father and stepmother and cared for them until they each passed away. His story points to the fact that, with God's help, we can overcome all of the vicissitudes of life. He went through situations that hampered his peace, joy, normal development, and education and suffered some of the worst forms of hatred and neglect. Still, even though he was just a young child, he kept close to God and worked hard, doing menial jobs, selling used clothing and other items involving laborious tasks, either to make a little money for himself or to serve the people who provided him help and shelter at the time. And he was able to succeed.

Early on in life, while going through his struggles, this man made Romans 8:37 his bedrock scripture:

Nay, in all these things, we are more than conquerors through him that loved us.

An interesting incident happened in his family while he was in college. His paternal grandmother, with whom he grew up during his early childhood years, became very ill and developed severe pain in one arm. The pain got increasingly worse, to the point that she could no longer rest or sleep. Nothing seemed to bring her relief.

When he went to visit her during his college break and saw what she was going through, he began fasting and praying, believing that whatever was wrong, the same God who was seeing him through his struggles was capable of granting the grandmother victory over her ordeal.

As the grandmother's situation got worse, every day he fasted and prayed and spoke the Word of God over her. One afternoon, while he was praying for his grandmother, she fell asleep and for the first time appeared comfortable in her rest, without the usual groaning and moaning. After some hours of sleep, the grandmother woke up. She had no more pain or discomfort and was in a very happy mood. The boy asked her what had happened, and she narrated to him a dream she had.

She said that she had fallen asleep during his prayer and had a dream. She saw a man. He was dressed all in white and was full of radiance. She tried to see his face but couldn't. He came walking into her room carrying some silver-looking surgical instruments in a silver-looking bowl and placed the bowl on the bed beside her. He then began to use the surgical instruments to cut through her arm. He removed a series of things that looked like wires from her arm. He placed them in the bowl. Then He sewed her arm back up, picked up the bowl, and walked out of the room.

It was then that she woke up and found that the pain she had been experiencing for many months was completely gone. Grandma was completely healed and delivered through the power of prayer, and the disease never returned. GLORY BE TO GOD!

THIS THIRD LEVEL IS THE LEVEL OF WALKING IN THE AUTHORITY OF A BELIEVER

Look at this truth from our Lord:

Behold, I give unto you power to tread on serpents and scorpions, and over all the power of the enemy: and nothing shall by any means hurt you.   Luke 10:19

A Christian who desires the sincere Word of God in Level 1 in order to grow and who submits to the leading of God in Level 2 (while continuing to desire the Word), will undoubtedly grow into Level 3 on the growth chart.

This is the level where the Christian is simply sold out to the efficacy of the Word of God: "Has God said it? Then I believe it—no matter what." This is the level of: "God said it; I believe it; and that settles it." Simply put, this is the level of complete stubborn faith in God and His Word. This is the level of understanding the Word of God and knowing that He does not lie and change His mind as human beings so often do:

> *God is not a man that he should lie; neither the son of man, that he should repent: hath he said, and shall he not do it? Or hath he spoken, and shall he not make it good?*
>
> Numbers 23:19

A Christian at this level is one who understands that although the devil may be on the way to hinder, God will surely and always give him or her victory. The enemy can never be so close to a child of God that God is not closer. When you know that you are never alone and that God is with you ALWAYS and ALWAY, fear begins to fade from your life and eventually becomes extinct. At the same time, faith rises in you.

Fear is a spirit and a huge weapon in the hand of the devil to bring down and destroy a Christian. Fear has torment and is capable of beating up any Christian at any level of growth, bringing them to the point of surrender (see 1 John 4:18).

The antidote to fear is faith, and faith comes from the Word of God. The psalmist said, *"I will fear no evil."* This was not because he could shoot a machine gun, not because he had Secret Service protection, not because he had connections with men in the upper echelons of business or the political world, not even because he had the right to own and bear arms, as American citizens do. Why, then? Because, he said, *"The LORD is with me."*

The psalmist David recognized that the presence of God was all he needed to overcome and defeat any and all forms of evil around him. He realized that even if Jesus appeared to be sleeping in the boat during a furious, violent, and fierce storm, with waves sweeping over and breaking into the boat, in the presence of this *"manner of man"* (Jesus, Matthew 8:23), the winds and the waves of life would always obey Him.

If you are in God's presence, it is impossible for you to drown from the storm. If you are in

His presence, it is impossible for you to perish from the storm. If you are in His presence, it is impossible for you to die from the storm. The antidote to the storm is the exercise of your faith:

Above all, taking the shield of faith, wherewith ye shall be able to quench all the fiery darts of the wicked. Ephesians 6:16

The Scriptures show that all Jesus did was get up and rebuke the winds and the waves, and it was suddenly completely calm. He expected the disciples to do the same, but fear and lack of faith would not let them:

Jesus responded, "Why are you afraid? You have so little faith!" Then he **GOT UP and REBUKED** *the wind and waves, and suddenly there was a great calm.*
Matthew 8:26, NLT (Emphasis Mine)

The devil cannot withstand a Christian who gets up and rebukes. The enemy cannot overcome a child of God who gets up and rebukes. The demons cannot conquer a believer who gets up and rebukes.

This is called the authority of the believer, and at this level on the growth chart, the child of God knows that we don't lie down, murmur, grumble and whine when the shadow of death shows up. Instead, we get up and we rebuke in the name of Jesus.

We don't operate in fear when the shadow of death shows up because *"Thou art with me."* We don't settle down in the valley of the shadow of death; we *"walk through"* it. Hallelujah! Praise the Lord God Almighty!

"SHEEP IN THE MIDST OF WOLVES"

Behold, I send you forth as sheep in the midst of wolves: be ye therefore wise as serpents, and harmless as doves. But beware of men: for they will deliver you up to the councils, and they will scourge you in their synagogues; and ye shall be brought before governors and kings for my sake, for a testimony against them and the Gentiles. But when they deliver you up, take no thought how or what ye shall speak: for it shall be given you in that same hour what ye shall speak. For it is not ye that speak, but the Spirit of your Father which speaketh in you.

Matthew 10:16-20

*These things I have spoken unto you, that in
me ye might have peace. In the world ye shall
have tribulation: but be of good cheer; I have
overcome the world.*   John 16:33

Our Lord Jesus did not hide the truth from
us. He told us very plainly that in this world
we *"shall have"* troubles. Our Shepherd taught
us that we are sheep in the midst of wolves.
We must beware of men who would beat us
and put us in danger because of our faith. We
are living in a world in which just our stand for
Jesus might cause people to hate us. But please
take note: You have already overcome all that
could possibly come against you.

Our Shepherd showed us the way to deal
with these things. First, we need to expect
them. If you are not expecting them, they will
overwhelm you when they come. Second,
we need to be wise in our approach to these
things. Act wisely in trials and temptations.

Our shepherd was wise when He was
tempted by Satan (see Matthew 4). He was wise
when He was tempted about paying taxes to
Caesar (see Mark 12:13-17). He was wise when
the Pharisees tempted Him about stoning the
woman caught in adultery (see John **8:3-9). He**

was wise when He was asked by a man to tell his brother to share with him the inheritance from their father (see Luke 12:13-14). Be wise, don't compromise and don't allow yourself to fall into men's traps.

At the same time, be harmless. Put on an uncompromising mindset, but approach everything with a tender heart of compassion and love for God and even for your persecutors. Our Lord Jesus taught us to love those who persecute us, pray for them, and even do good to them:

Ye have heard that it hath been said, Thou shalt love thy neighbour, and hate thine enemy. But I say unto you, Love your enemies, bless them that curse you, do good to them that hate you, and pray for them which despitefully use you, and persecute you; that ye may be the children of your Father which is in heaven: for he maketh his sun to rise on the evil and on the good, and sendeth rain on the just and on the unjust. For if ye love them which love you, what reward have ye? do not even the publicans the same? And if ye salute your brethren only, what do ye more than others? do not even the publicans so? Be ye therefore perfect, even as your Father which is in heaven is perfect.

Matthew 5:43-48

GOD'S PRESENCE IS THE ULTIMATE DECIDING FACTOR

God's presence is the ultimate deciding factor in the valley of the shadow of death. The psalmist said, *"For thou art with me."* Let's take a moment to digest what His presence means and does in our lives:

His presence roots out fear:

Fear thou not; for I am with thee.

Isaiah 41:10

The LORD is on my side; I will not fear: what can man do unto me? Psalm 118:6

His presence roots out failure:

Be strong and of good courage, fear not, nor be afraid of them: for the LORD thy God, he it is that doth go with thee; he will not fail thee, nor forsake thee. Deuteronomy 31:6

His presence brings the joy of salvation:

The LORD thy God in the midst of thee is mighty; he will save, he will rejoice over thee with joy; he will rest in his love, he will joy over thee with singing.   Zephaniah 3:17

His presence is His promise to His children:

Have not I commanded thee? Be strong and of a good courage; be not afraid, neither be thou dismayed: for the LORD thy God is with thee whithersoever thou goest.   Joshua 1:9

Behold, a virgin shall be with child, and shall bring forth a son, and they shall call his name Emmanuel, which being interpreted is, God with us.   Matthew 1:23

Teaching them to observe all things whatsoever I have commanded you: and, lo, I am with you always, even unto the end of the world. Amen!   Matthew 28:20

Let your conversation be without covetousness; and be content with such things as ye

have: for he hath said, I will never leave thee,
nor forsake thee.   Hebrews 13:5

We need to believe that our Shepherd will not leave us in the valley of the shadow of death. This Shepherd laid down his life for His sheep. If He could lay down His life for us, what could He not do for us?

It is very important for the Christian to know how to cultivate God's presence in the midst of trials and temptations. Our Lord Jesus Christ prayed and fasted. He told Peter and the rest of the disciples to pray that they enter not into temptation (see Matthew 26:41). He told Peter that Satan wanted to sift him like wheat but that He had prayed for him (see Luke 22:31-32).

Watch out, child of God! The valley of the shadow of death is a real place, there is a real devil who would like to sift you like wheat, and there are temptations all around you. Watch! Pray! Fast! Use God's Word! Put on faith! I believe that this will cultivate the presence of God around you, enabling you to overcome every trial of your faith.

Note that it is in the place of the shadow of death experience that the Christian is taught the truth about the Shepherd's rod and staff. He now learns that both God's rod and staff are instruments of teaching and guidance. He learns that the rod of God is not to kill but to correct:

> *The* LORD *hath chastened me sore: but he hath not given me over unto death.* Psalm 118:18

He learns that the rod of God is employed out of His great love:

> *For whom the Lord loveth he chasteneth, and scourgeth every son whom he receiveth.*
> Hebrews 12:6

> *For whom the* LORD *loveth he correcteth; even as a father the son in whom he delighteth.*
> Proverbs 3:12

He learns that the rod of God is a symbol of His divine guidance and care, not just for punishment and correction. God, by using His rod, helps His children navigate their way through and out of the valley of the shadow of death.

In the same valley of the shadow of death, the Christian also learns that the staff of God, although it signifies position and authority, should never be used as an instrument of pride but rather of teaching, guidance, and care.

God provides His staff to guide us and not to evoke or draw out pride in us. To the children of the world, the staff is a means to intimidate others, but to the Kingdom child, the staff of God is an instrument of guidance. To the children of the world, the staff brings pride, but to the child of God, the staff brings humility. We are not of the world. The Scriptures admonish us: *"Come out from among them and be ye separate"*:

Wherefore come out from among them, and be ye separate, saith the Lord, and touch not the unclean thing; and I will receive you. And will be a father unto you, and ye shall be my sons and daughters, saith the Lord Almighty.
2 Corinthians 6:17-18

Let the Shepherd's rod and staff perform the work of comfort in you and not of shame, guilt, and pride.

At this level of Christian growth, what determines your graduation to the next level is simple faith and humility. To grow into the next level on the growth chart, the child of God must add faith and humility to the quality of desire on Level 1 and the quality of submission on Level 2. May God strengthen your faith and keep you humble as you run this race in Jesus' mighty name. Amen!

CHAPTER FOUR

LOCATING YOUR PLACE IN MINISTRY

Verse 5:
Thou preparest a table before me in the presence of mine enemies: thou anointest my head with oil; my cup runneth over.

PSALM 23

LEVEL 5—HIS ULTIMATE MANIFESTED PRESENCE

— VERSE 6 —
Surely goodness and mercy shall follow me all the days of my life; and I will dwell in the house of the Lord forever.

— VERSE 5 —
Thou preparest a table before me in the presence of mine enemies; thou anointest my head with oil; my cup runneth over.

LEVEL 4—LOCATING YOUR PLACE IN THE MINISTRY

— VERSE 4 —
Yea, though I walk through the valley of the shadow of death, I will fear no evil: for thou art with me; thy rod and thy staff they comfort me.

LEVEL 3—OPERATING IN THE AUTHORITY OF A BELIEVER

— VERSE 3 —
He restoreth my soul: he leadeth me in the paths of righteousness for his name's sake.

LEVEL 2—TAKING ON HIS IDENTITY

— VERSE 2 —
He maketh me to lie down in green pastures: he leadeth me beside the still waters.

LEVEL 1—NEWBORN BABE

The Table God Prepares for Us

A table is a platform from which you perform your functions. A table is meant to provide a level surface on which objects are placed and functions are carried out. God's table is meant to provide a state of physical and spiritual balance as you carry out His assignment. As tables are of different styles, shapes, and sizes, God prepares specific platforms for us, depending on His assignment and calling. Then He anoints (equips) us to perform and operate on that platform.

Different tables perform different functions. Understanding your table (platform) is very important and necessary to fulfilling your God-designed purpose in life. I don't have to minister or preach like some senior pastor because tables and platforms are different. I don't have to have the same mega following as an archbishop because tables and platforms are different. I don't have to receive the same accolades as a bishop because tables and platforms are indeed different.

My fulfilment lies in identifying and operating in God's specific, divine table (platform) for me. The growth and success of my ministry lies in operating in God's specifically and divinely designed table (platform) for me.

Don't be tempted into preparing your own table (platform) because you envy the platform of a senior pastor, a bishop, or an archbishop. Such tables don't last once exposed to the attacks of the enemy, but the table God prepares withstands all of the wiles of the enemy.

A key factor in the making of a table is stability. Tables are built to be stable, and the more stable the table is, the greater the efficiency of its use. A table that is wobbly and shaky is a table that is faulty, and God cannot produce faulty outcomes. The Scriptures say:

I know that everything God does will endure forever.　　　　　Ecclesiastes 3:14, NIV

Thou preparest a table before me.　Psalm 23:5

It is not the plan of God for anyone to be unstable in ministry. It cannot be God who introduced instability into your service to Him in the fulfilment of divine purpose. God's table (platform) is stable, and any form of instability that you experience is not His doing.

Most instability in life is the result of a curse from man or the devil, or it may be self-inflicted. Jacob cursed his son Reuben:

Unstable as water, thou shalt not excel; because thou wentest up to thy father's bed; then defiledst thou it: he went up to my couch. Genesis 49:4

Instability in life and ministry is meant by the enemy primarily to hinder your success and ensure that you don't excel in your God-given assignments.

- James 1:8 tells us that doublemindedness can make you unstable.
- Matthew 7:26-27 says that hearing and not acting on the Word of God can make your work unstable.
- Ephesians 4:14 shows that a Christian who is not growing becomes unstable.
- 2 Peter 3:16 says that it is the unstable who distort the Scriptures.
- 2 Peter 2:14 says that unstable souls are easily enticed.

The plan of God is that you be stable in your God-given assignment:

Therefore, my beloved brethren, be steadfast, immovable [stable], *always abounding in the work of the Lord, knowing that your toil* [assignment] *is not in vain in the Lord.*

1 Corinthians 15:58

If indeed you continue in the faith [assignment], *firmly established* [stable] *and steadfast, not moved away from the hope of the gospel that you have heard.*

Colossians 1:23, NKJV

The Lord prepares a table (platform) before me, in the open, not in secret. The table the Lord prepares for me is a stable platform, but that which is prepared by man (including me and you) is destined for instability and will hinder you from excelling in the work God has assigned to you.

HE ANOINTS MY HEAD WITH OIL

Notice that the Lord prepares the table in the open (in the presence of even my enemies), but He anoints (equips) me in the secret place (the closet, the quarry, the alone place with God), to function and excel in the service of the table (platform) openly. The anointing

God provides will take you to the top and will surely get the work done anytime, every time, anywhere, and everywhere.

Let's take a look at the befogging phenomenon the Bible describes in the building of the Temple:

> *And the house, when it was in building, was built of stones made ready before it was brought thither: so that there was neither hammer nor axe nor any tool of iron heard in the house, while it was in building.* 1 Kings 6:7

I used the phrase *befogging phenomenon* because I have never in my fifty years of existence on this earth seen a building with work in progress without any sound of equipment being heard during active construction. Note here that this is not talking about a city where everyone was deaf. The Bible is actually talking about a city where people could hear, and yet they heard no sound of equipment while the building of the Temple was in progress. The reason, the Bible says, is because the stones used for this building were prepared elsewhere, at a quarry. From there, they were brought to the construction site and fit perfectly into the areas of the structure they were meant to occupy — round pegs in round holes, square pegs in square holes — fitted perfectly without need for hammer, chisel, or any other iron tool.

"Thou preparest a table" — a platform, a podium, a pulpit, a rostrum, a floor, or an arena — before me, openly, in the presence of my enemies. Then God goes behind the scene, at the quarry, to anoint, consecrate, sanctify, chisel, and form me to His exact specification for the prepared platform. Every child of God is a statue formed in the secret place, to fit an openly-constructed base or platform.

God, not man, prepares the platform. God brings His man to mentor you for that platform. The platform is not prepared by you, O child of God. The platform is not prepared by your bishop, O man of God. And certainly, it is not prepared by your parent, O Kingdom children.

God knows the size, shape, weight, and dimensions of the platform He wants you to operate on, and He alone can anoint, prepare, and equip you to operate perfectly on it. Otherwise there is bound to be a lot of noise in your ministry and in your walk with and work for the Lord.

What a lot of ministries are experiencing in these days is noise. Yes, many noisemakers, not ministers of God, have risen to occupy platforms that were not prepared by God for them. Either God prepared the platform and they schemed out the one fit for the platform, or they simply went ahead and constructed the platform by themselves. This explains why there is so much noise and so little results in the church today.

The church is seeing more and more hammers, chisels, and other iron tools being used in ministry and very little of anointing because the man of God, represented by the statue, was not prepared by God in the quarry to fit the platform he is operating on. There has to be continuous hammering and chiseling at the construction site, thereby producing noise and not the anointing, because these people were not prepared in the quarry.

We now see many men and women of God leading multitudes in a way God never instructed. We see the words of the men of God having less and less impact in building godly character in their followers. The church is now full of noisemakers instead of anointed servants of God. The key factor of a successful walk with God is the anointing, and God has reserved this for lovers of righteousness and haters of wickedness:

> *Thou lovest righteousness and hated wickedness: therefore God, thy God, hast anointed thee with the oil of gladness above thy fellows.*
>
> Psalm 45:7

John the Baptist spent thirty years in the quarry being prepared for a ministry platform that he executed perfectly in about six months, and yet John the Baptist, although gone now for more than two thousand years, left a trail that not one of us has been able to replicate.

Jesus spent thirty years in the quarry being prepared for a ministry platform He successfully discharged in three years, yet Jesus, although gone now in body for more than two thousand years, left a work that none of us has been able to replicate, even though He left us the calling and the anointing to do *"greater works"*:

> *Verily, verily, I say unto you, he that believeth on me, the works that I do shall he do also; and*

*greater works than these shall he do; because I
go unto my Father.*   John 14:12

The reason for this lack of real transform-
ing godly impact in ministry lies in the failure
to allow God to put us in the exact shape that
fits the exact platform He built for us as indi-
viduals in the Kingdom of God. We all want to
pray, preach, and function like other men and
women of God, without having a clue how
God carved them out to fit the respective platforms they occupy today.

The Scriptures say:

*Ephraim compromises with the nations; he's
a half-baked cake.*   Hosea 7:8, ISV

Some translations compare Ephraim to a
half-baked loaf of bread, and some compare
him to a flat loaf not turned over. Have you
not seen that a whole lot of men and women of
God have one side that taste so good, like cake
fully baked, and yet when the other side is revealed, they resemble a cake that has not yet
seen the grill or oven. In fact, they reveal the
absence of God to the extent that it frightens
and shocks every true child of God.

Look at these different versions of 2 Peter 2:3:

And through covetousness shall they with feigned words make merchandise of you. KJV

By covetousness they will exploit you with deceptive words. NKJV

In their greed, these false teachers will exploit you with deceptive words. BSB

Anointed men and women of God do not engage in exploitation of the children of God. Anointed men or women of God are a conduit through which God delivers and saves His children from the path of Hell and damnation.

So the questions now are:

- What table are you operating on?
- Do you know the purpose of that table?
- Who prepared the table?
- And have you been anointed by God to operate on that table?

If you truly have been anointed to operate on God's table specifically designed for you, and you understand and follow the purpose for which God placed you on that platform, then no devil from the pit of Hell can stop your cup from running over in the name of Jesus Christ. No devil from the pit of Hell can stop you from having more than enough for your needs in Jesus' mighty name. The Word of God declares:

"MY CUP RUNNETH OVER!"

So shall your case be, in Jesus' mighty name. Amen!

To remain at this level on the growth chart and eventually progress into the next and final level, the child of God must operate in the knowledge, understanding, and wisdom of God.

So, along these stages of growth of a believer, we learn that the child of God requires certain qualities if he or she is to successfully mature in his or her walk with God. The qualities identified include: desire, submission, faith, and humility, and now knowledge, understanding, and wisdom.

MY TABLE IN THE PRESENCE OF MY ENEMIES

We need to understand that God prepares a table before us in the presence of our enemies. The Lord has not promised us the absence of enemies. If He, being our Lord and Savior, had enemies, and a servant is not greater than his Lord, we, too, will have enemies:

> *If the world hate you, ye know that it hated me before it hated you. If ye were of the world, the world would love his own: but because ye are not of the world, but I have chosen you out of the world, therefore the world hateth you. Remember the word that I said unto you, The servant is not greater than his lord. If they have persecuted me, they will also persecute you; if they have kept my saying, they will keep yours also.* John 15:18-20

God always provides a feast for us, even in the midst of our enemies, and He does it to shame those enemies. Let us be assured that God can provide in the midst of opposition and challenges. There will be opposition, but we need to understand that our Father is greater than any and all of it. Storms and opposition are opportunities for the manifestation of the blessings and promises of God.

Many have been called into ministry in challenging times and under challenging circumstances. Some discover their ministry at a time of tragedy in their family or a health, financial, or other challenge they may have encountered. In the darkest hour is when God's light shines brightest. Our Lord Jesus came to a people who dwell in darkness:

The people that walked in darkness have seen a great light: they that dwell in the land of the shadow of death, upon them hath the light shined.   Isaiah 9:2

So, let us remember that there is always an enemy present where there is a table of blessing. Overcome the enemy and enjoy the blessing in Jesus' name.

CHAPTER FIVE

HIS ULTIMATE MANIFESTED PRESENCE

Verse 6:
Surely goodness and mercy shall follow me all the days of my life: and I will dwell in the house of the LORD forever.

PSALM 23

LEVEL 5—HIS ULTIMATE MANIFESTED PRESENCE

— VERSE 6 —
Surely goodness and mercy shall follow me all the days of my life: and I will dwell in the house of the Lord forever.

— VERSE 5 —
Thou preparest a table before me in the presence of mine enemies: thou anointest my head with oil; my cup runneth over.

LEVEL 4—LOCATING YOUR PLACE IN THE MINISTRY

— VERSE 4 —
Yea, though I walk through the valley of the shadow of death, I will fear no evil: for thou art with me; thy rod and thy staff they comfort me.

LEVEL 3—OPERATING IN THE AUTHORITY OF A BELIEVER

— VERSE 3 —
He restoreth my soul: he leadeth me in the paths of righteousness for his name's sake.

LEVEL 2—TAKING ON HIS IDENTITY

— VERSE 2 —
He maketh me to lie down in green pastures: he leadeth me beside the still waters.

LEVEL 1—NEWBORN BABE

SURELY AND FOREVER

The ultimate goal of a child of God is to
dwell in the presence of God, both here and
in the life hereafter. This verse is the climax of
our walk with God. It is the finish line of our
race, the final location of our journey, the apex
of our climbing:

> *One thing have I desired of the* LORD, *that
> will I seek after; that I may dwell in the house
> of the* LORD *all the days of my life, to behold
> the beauty of the* LORD, *and to inquire in his
> temple.*   Psalm 27:4

First, there are two key words worth looking into in this 6th verse of Psalm 23. They
are the words *SURELY* and *FOREVER*. The
word *surely* is used to emphasize strong belief
that what has been spoken is true and should
leave no doubt. *Surely* provides assurance and
confidence. This is not self-confidence, but the
confidence that comes only from God. God is
true, God is trustworthy, and God is reliable:

> *God is not human, that he should lie,
> not a human being, that he should change his
> mind.*

Does he speak and then not act?
Does he promise and not fulfill?

Numbers 23:19, NIV

The word *forever* implies "a lasting or permanent state." It connotes continuity and eternity, it represents all future times, and it explains an "ALWAYS" kind of situation and circumstance. The 6th verse of this psalm, therefore, describes the certainty and the continuity of the plan of God for every believer.

Jesus, speaking to His disciples, said:

If it were not so, I would have told you.

John 14:2

God's Word can be trusted. God's Word never fails. He says what He means and means what He says. Truth is one of His attributes:

I will worship toward thy holy temple, and praise thy name for your lovingkindness and for thy truth; for thou hast magnified thy word above all thy name. Psalm 138:2

God's Attributes in Permanent Manifestation

This final level on the growth chart of a

believer is where God's attributes are in permanent visible manifestation in the life of a child of God. This is where God's attributes of goodness and mercy come alive and take up permanent residence in our lives.

Goodness is that which meets our every need, and mercy is that which provides assurance that we are forgiven. Goodness demonstrates the hand of God, while mercy demonstrates the heart of God. Both attributes are here represented by living beings; they move, they walk, and they follow us wherever we go. Charles Spurgeon described them as "two heavenly messengers." This is detailed in the words of the psalmist:

For the Lord *is* **GOOD***; his* **MERCY** *is* **EVERLASTING***; and his* **TRUTH** **ENDURETH** *to all generations.*
                    Psalm 100:5 (Emphasis Mine)

This scripture encapsulates the words *goodness, mercy, surely,* and *forever.* Praise God!

Jehovah is inherently good, merciful, and true to all who put their trust in Him. These attributes are built-in, inborn, inbred, immanent, stuck in Him so firmly that they can never be separated.

Jesus, describing the Kingdom of Heaven in Matthew 20, warned against judging the goodness of God by the possessions of those around you. He explained that God is faithful and true to His promise, no matter how lopsided we think things may seem in the natural:

But he answered one of them, and said, Friend, I do thee no wrong: didst not thou agree with me for a penny? Matthew 20:13

Is it not lawful for me to do that I will with mine own? Is thine eye evil, because I am good? Matthew 20:15

The goodness of God manifested in the life of man causes the radiance of God's presence to be seen:

And he said, I beseech thee, shew me thy glory. And he said, I will make all my GOODNESS pass before thee.
Exodus 33:18-19 (Emphasis Mine)

Moses asked to see the glory of God, but God said to him, "I will show you something rather capable of making your face to glow.

I will show you My GOODNESS," and the outcome was seen when Moses returned to the people. When he came down from Mount Sinai with the two tablets of the covenant law in his hands, he was not aware that his face was radiant because he had spoken with the Lord. Others saw it:

When Aaron and all the Israelites saw Moses, his face was radiant, and they were afraid to come near him. Exodus 34:30, NIV

Again I say that the goodness of God manifested in the life of a man causes the radiance of God's presence to be seen in his life. Goodness is shown as both the character and the actions of God:

You are good, and what you do is good. Psalm 119:68, NIV

God is good in and of Himself. He is the true definition of goodness.

Secondly, the true character of a person is seen by his or her actions. Look at this scripture:

How God anointed Jesus of Nazareth with the Holy Spirit and power, and how He went around doing GOOD and healing all who were under the power of the devil, because God was with him.   Acts 10:38, NIV
(Emphasis Mine)

The entire Bible is a chronicle of God's actions and work in the lives of His people. These actions demonstrate His lovingkind-ness, his tender mercies, His forgiveness, His grace, His protection, and so on. Even in the realm of His thoughts, God is still good to us.

This is remarkable because even the best of men, while doing things to demonstrate good to you, will still often harbor bad thoughts toward you. As a matter of fact, I wouldn't want to know what the thoughts are toward me even of someone who is doing physical good to me. This is not so with God:

"For I know the plans [thoughts] *I have for you," says the* LORD. *"They are plans* [thoughts] *for good and not for disaster, to give you a future and a hope."*
Jeremiah 29:11, NLT

In spite of our fallen nature, God still loved us while we were yet sinners. He gave His only begotten Son to die on the cross to forgive us of our sins and to reconcile us back to Himself. He still patiently stands at the door of our sinful hearts and knocks, imploring us to open, so that He can have a relationship with us — a relationship we stand to benefit from.

God is good to us, not because we are nice people. His goodness is meant to lead us to Himself:

> *Don't you see how wonderfully kind, tolerant, and patient God is with you? Does this mean nothing to you? Can't you see that His kindness* [goodness] *is intended to turn you from your sin?* Romans 2:4, NLT

Now, in case you believe that God is good but are still wondering if He will be good to you in every area of your life, in case you believe that all good and perfect gifts come from Him, and you actually have seen the goodness of God in the lives of those around you, the question is: Do you believe that God is good to you all the time?

Jesus said:

My purpose is to give them a rich and satisfy-ing life.   John 10:10, NLT

God cannot lie. In fact, the Bible states:

It was IMPOSSIBLE for God to lie.
        Hebrews 6:18, NLT (Emphasis Mine)

This, therefore, means that the proof of God's goodness in your life is in the tasting:

Taste and see that the LORD is GOOD.
        Psalm 34:8, NLT (Emphasis Mine)

- To taste, you must return to Him.
- To taste, you must accept Him into your life as your personal Lord and Savior.
- To taste, you must make Him your Shepherd.
- To taste, you must allow Him to restore your soul.
- To taste, you must allow Him to lead and guide you in the paths of righteousness.
- To taste, you must yield to His rod and staff as His instruments of comfort and not pun-ishment and pride.
- To taste, you must allow Him to be the One

who prepares your table (platform), according to His will and purpose for your life.

• To taste, you must sincerely and consistently seek His anointing in a place of fellowship and worship.

The ultimate goal of a successful Christian is a place of eternity with the Lord:

AND I WILL DWELL IN THE HOUSE OF THE LORD, FOR EVER!

This, to me, is not the typical church service, even if your church holds services every day of the week. This, to me, is not your typical prayer meeting, even if you hold these meetings every day of the week. As good as your personal time with God may be, this, to me, still is not your typical personal time of fellowship with the Lord.

As a matter of fact, concerning those meetings we mention here, it doesn't matter how long you spend in worship, you still can't reach the state of FOREVER in the House of the Lord.

The climax of the Christian race is one and only one thing: being accepted into God's eternal presence, when your work here on earth is done or being among those who are *"caught up together in the clouds to meet the Lord in the air"* if Christ returns while you are still alive (1 Thessalonians 4:17, NIV).

This should be the ultimate desire of every child of God:

> *One thing I ask from the* LORD,
> *this only do I seek:*
> *that I may dwell in the house of the* LORD
> *all the days of my life,*
> *to gaze on the beauty of the* LORD
> *and to seek him in his temple.*
>
> Psalm 27:4, NIV

THERE IS A CITY OF GOD

Young Christians today, for the most part, don't yet understand that there is life after this life, that life is eternal, and that life will be lived in either one of two places: the city of God or a place of torment:

> *And it came to pass, that the beggar died, and was carried by the angels into Abraham's bosom: the rich man also died, and was buried; and in hell he lift up his eyes, being in*

torments, and seeth Abraham afar off, and Lazarus in His bosom. Luke 16:22-23

There is a city of God, no matter what your philosophical views are as either a Christian or a non-Christian. The Scriptures clearly say that THERE IS A CITY OF GOD. Jesus said:

My Father's house has many rooms; if that were not so, would I have told you that I am going there to prepare a place for you?
John 14:2, NIV

There is a city of God. The Scriptures, speaking of Abraham, say:

By faith Abraham, when he was called to go out into a place which he should after receive for an inheritance, obeyed; and he went out, not knowing whither he went. By faith he so-journed in the land of promise, as in a strange country, dwelling in tabernacles with Isaac and Jacob, the heirs with him of the same promise. FOR HE LOOKED FOR A CITY WHICH HATH FOUNDATIONS, WHOSE BUILDER AND MAKER IS GOD.
Hebrews 11:8-10 (Emphasis Mine)

Yes, there is a city of God:

And I John saw the holy city, new Jerusalem, coming down from God out of heaven, prepared as a bride adorned for her husband.
Revelation 21:2

There is a city of God:

But now they desire a better country, that is, an heavenly: wherefore God is not ashamed to be called their God: for he hath prepared for them a city. Hebrews 11:16

There is a city of God:

For here we do not have a permanent city, but we are looking for the city that is to come.
Hebrews 13:14, BSB

There is a city of God:

Great is the LORD, and greatly to be praised in THE CITY OF OUR GOD, in the mountain of his holiness.
Psalm 48:1 (Emphasis Mine)

There is a city of God:

There is a river, the streams whereof shall make glad THE CITY OF GOD, the holy place of the tabernacles of the most High. Psalm 46:4

Paul wrote:

I have fought a good fight, I have finished my course, I have kept the faith: henceforth there is laid up for me a crown of righteousness, which the Lord, the righteous judge, shall give me at that day: and not to me only, but unto all them also that love his appearing.
2 Timothy 4:7-8

Three things Christians need to know and do in order to climax in God's eternal presence are:

1. Fight the fight of faith,
2. Fight to the end, and
3. Fight in total obedience to the Word of the Great Shepherd.

The climax of this chapter of the Bible describes where the born-again, Spirit-filled, obedient child of God is meant to dwell: IN THE PRESENCE OF THE LORD, in this life and in the life eternal, and the responsibility of the sheep here is total worship and praise.

SUMMARY

Now here is a summary of this 23rd Psalm:

Verse 2

He maketh me ... he leadeth me.

Verse 3

He restoreth my soul. ... he leadeth me [again, after falling and after restoration].

Verse 4

"Thou art with me" (implies that He is present).
"Thy rod and staff" (implies that He comforts me).

Verse 5

"He prepareth a table" implies that He gives me a platform. *"Thou anointest my head"* implies that He equips me to perform and operate on that platform.

Making Before Leading

"HE MAKETH ME," in verse 2, implies that there is a making before there can be a leading. You cannot be led if you are not first made. In Genesis 2:8, God planted (prepared) a garden (a platform) east of Eden, and there (in the garden) He put (placed) the man He had formed (made). Note that the man He placed in the garden was the man He had formed, not a man He had not yet formed. Many wonder why they are not operating at a higher level of grace and anointing. The answer is in "the making." The platform is designed by God for the man (or woman) He has made.

Notice this Progression

There is a making first; then He leads the one He made in safety (verse 2). In the event there is a fall and then a willingness to get back up, He restores the soul and continues to lead (verse 3), more so now, in the path of righteousness, to prevent another fall.

God, because of His utmost goal to build (prepare) a platform for us and to equip (anoint) us to operate on that platform (verse 5), allows us to witness the shadows of death (verse 4). He allows the storms to show up. He allows the wind to be furious. He allows even the enemy to buffet us. But in and through it all, He maintains His divine presence so that the rivers cannot drown us, the fires cannot burn us, the flames cannot consume us. Praise God! His truth endures forever.

When thou passest through the waters, I will be with thee; and through the rivers, they shall not overflow thee: when thou walkest through the fire, thou shalt not be burned; neither shall the flame kindle upon thee. Isaiah 43:2

That s the promise of the Good Shepherd.

Conclusion

The Christian Growth Chart

I. Infant Stage

The LORD is my shepherd; I shall not want. He maketh me to lie down in green pastures: he leadeth me beside the still waters.

Who the Shepherd is to you and what you must do:

The Shepherd:
- *He is Lord.*
- *He is the Provider.*
- *He nurtures.*
- *He leads.*

The Sheep:
- *He lies down.*
- *He feeds.*

- *He desires.*
- *He grows.*

II. ADOLESCENCE

He restoreth my soul: he leadeth me in paths of righteousness for his name's sake.

Who the Shepherd is to you and what you must do:

The Shepherd:
- *He restores.*
- *He leads.*

The Sheep:
- *He develops a sense of responsibility.*
- *He must follow in paths of wisdom, righteousness, holiness, and redemption.*
- *He must walk in Christ's image.*

III. AGE FOR WAR

Though I walk through the valley of the shadow of death, I will fear no evil: for thou art with me; thy rod and thy staff they comfort me.

Who the Shepherd is to you and what you must do:

The Shepherd:
- *He never leaves or forsakes you.*
- *His rod and His staff comfort you.*

The Sheep:
- *He walks in valleys and shadows of death.*
- *To him, the rod and staff are instruments of comfort.*
- *He is an overcomer.*
- *He has no fear.*
- *He is assured of the presence of the Shepherd.*

IV. TIME FOR MINISTRY

Thou prepares a table before me in the presence of mine enemies: thou anointest my head with oil; my cup runneth over.

Who the Shepherd is to you and what you must do:

The Shepherd:
- *He prepares a table for you.*
- *He anoints your head with oil.*
- *He provides an overflow.*

The Sheep:
- He stays at the table prepared for him.
- He stays in his anointing.
- He remains aware of enemies.

V. Climaxing Your Walk with God Forever

Surely goodness and mercy shall follow me all the days of my life: and I will dwell in the house of the Lord *for ever.*

Who the Shepherd is to you and what you must do:

The Shepherd:
- *His presence is assured.*
- *His mercies and goodness are assured.*
- *Eternity with Him is assured.*

The Sheep:
- *He must receive God's presence.*
- *He must receive God's goodness and mercies.*
- *He must dwell in God's house forever.*

Now, in closing:

Now, may the LORD *bless you and keep you;*
May the LORD *make his face to shine on you and be gracious to you;*
May the LORD *turn his face toward you and give you peace; now and forever.*

Amen!

A Testimonial

Wow! What a lovely book with deep and practical insights into the growth process of a believer from the toddler level to a valiant man or woman of war in the Kingdom, now operating with the authority and power of Christ, and entering into the overflowing goodness and blessings of God. The scriptures and testimonies in this anointed book blessed my heart greatly.

I highly recommend this book for every believer and for pastors globally to provide to their congregations. It is very good Christian literature for the discipleship of new converts and also for established believers in Christ.

Pastor Emmanuel Umosen is a highly anointed and precious man of God. I have known him since March 2008 when I just relocated to the United States from Nigeria. From the first day I heard him minister in worship and in the preaching of the Word of faith, my heart was knitted to his spirit. I saw a man on fire, set ablaze for God. When I am privileged to be under his ministrations in church or via his weekly teleconference prayer line, every statement he makes carries the life of God and is very prophetic. I get the Word in season for my life every time I hear him minister. He is an anointed teacher and preacher of the Word of God with precision.

Pastor Umosen is very versed and loaded with the Word of life. You can never be bored for a second listening to him preach or teach. Never! I always learn a new scripture when I hear him. When he leads prayers after his ministrations, my body literally vibrates, and the whole atmosphere is set on fire. You can feel God's mighty presence. It is so palpable.

Pastor Umosen's prayer and fasting life is another great inspiration to me and a multitude of believers around the globe. He is also an anointed seer or prophet and operates effortlessly with the revelation gifts of the Holy Spirit (the word of knowledge, the word of wisdom, and discerning of spirits).

I and members of the Winners Chapel Int'l Kansas City saw a full manifestation of his prophetic office when we were privileged to have him minister to us on October 17, 2017 at our Covenant Day of Fruitfulness Service. It was his first time in Kansas City. At the hotel before coming over to the service, he gave a word of prophecy to the front desk staff, and she broke down in tears on her knees and received his counsel and blessings. She told me privately that if he was staying for a few days, she would make it free. That doesn't happen in America, but that is what the anointing does.

While at the service, he preached the Word with great light and illumination and suddenly switched into the prophetic when he called out people who needed the fruit of the womb. One of the women already had a child but needed another child. He saw that in the Spirit and said, "I hear 'proper child'." Then he told her "take it." She conceived that same month and delivered a beautiful princess in nine months exactly. I never told him about anyone in our church, I didn't even tell him of the career battles and stagnation I was facing at the time.

Here is the most striking manifestation of his prophetic office that almost brought me to tears. A lady stood in for her sister in London who had been married for eight years and had suffered repeated miscarriages. She came forward for prayer with her sister's picture. Pastor Umosen prayed in tongues briefly and saw in the realm of the Spirit an altar of darkness where a goat was slaughtered repeatedly up to eight times, which led to the multiple miscarriages. The lady broke down in tears on her knees, and screamed, "She has had eight miscarriages." This lady had never told me of this before, and this was Pastor Umosen's first time seeing her. I gained greater respect for the grace of God upon him from that day.

I knew he had paid the heavy price of relentless prayer and fasting over the years and a sanctified walk with God, to enter into the supernatural realm of seeing and hearing in the realm of the Spirit.

I am so honored to know this precious servant of God, a member of God's Army. His lovely wife is also a woman with fire in her bones and is a great helpmeet for God's general.

Pastor Esosa Ighodaro
Winners Chapel Kansas City
Missouri, USA

AUTHOR CONTACT PAGE

You may communicate directly with Pastor Emmanuel Umosen in the following ways:

Pastor Emmanuel Umosen
HOUSE OF PRAYER EVANGELISTIC (HOPE) MINISTRIES
940 W. FM 544
P.O. Box 833
Wylie, TX 75098
USA

eMail: hope.outcomes@gmail.com
eumosen@gmail.com

AND SAMUEL
GREW, AND THE
LORD WAS WITH
HIM, AND DID
LET NONE OF HIS
WORDS FALL TO THE
GROUND.

— 1 SAMUEL 3:19